C-1540   CAREER EXAMINATION SERIES

This is your
PASSBOOK for...

Youth Group Supervisor

Test Preparation Study Guide
Questions & Answers

COPYRIGHT NOTICE

This book is SOLELY intended for, is sold ONLY to, and its use is RESTRICTED to individual, bona fide applicants or candidates who qualify by virtue of having seriously filed applications for appropriate license, certificate, professional and/or promotional advancement, higher school matriculation, scholarship, or other legitimate requirements of education and/or governmental authorities.

This book is NOT intended for use, class instruction, tutoring, training, duplication, copying, reprinting, excerption, or adaptation, etc., by:

1) Other publishers
2) Proprietors and/or Instructors of "Coaching" and/or Preparatory Courses
3) Personnel and/or Training Divisions of commercial, industrial, and governmental organizations
4) Schools, colleges, or universities and/or their departments and staffs, including teachers and other personnel
5) Testing Agencies or Bureaus
6) Study groups which seek by the purchase of a single volume to copy and/or duplicate and/or adapt this material for use by the group as a whole without having purchased individual volumes for each of the members of the group
7) Et al.

Such persons would be in violation of appropriate Federal and State statutes.

PROVISION OF LICENSING AGREEMENTS – Recognized educational, commercial, industrial, and governmental institutions and organizations, and others legitimately engaged in educational pursuits, including training, testing, and measurement activities, may address request for a licensing agreement to the copyright owners, who will determine whether, and under what conditions, including fees and charges, the materials in this book may be used them. In other words, a licensing facility exists for the legitimate use of the material in this book on other than an individual basis. However, it is asseverated and affirmed here that the material in this book CANNOT be used without the receipt of the express permission of such a licensing agreement from the Publishers. Inquiries re licensing should be addressed to the company, attention rights and permissions department.

All rights reserved, including the right of reproduction in whole or in part, in any form or by any means, electronic or mechanical, including photocopying, recording, or by any information storage and retrieval system, without permission in writing from the Publisher.

Copyright © 2025 by
National Learning Corporation

212 Michael Drive, Syosset, NY 11791
(516) 921-8888 • www.passbooks.com
E-mail: info@passbooks.com

PASSBOOK® SERIES

THE *PASSBOOK® SERIES* has been created to prepare applicants and candidates for the ultimate academic battlefield – the examination room.

At some time in our lives, each and every one of us may be required to take an examination – for validation, matriculation, admission, qualification, registration, certification, or licensure.

Based on the assumption that every applicant or candidate has met the basic formal educational standards, has taken the required number of courses, and read the necessary texts, the *PASSBOOK® SERIES* furnishes the one special preparation which may assure passing with confidence, instead of failing with insecurity. Examination questions – together with answers – are furnished as the basic vehicle for study so that the mysteries of the examination and its compounding difficulties may be eliminated or diminished by a sure method.

This book is meant to help you pass your examination provided that you qualify and are serious in your objective.

The entire field is reviewed through the huge store of content information which is succinctly presented through a provocative and challenging approach – the question-and-answer method.

A climate of success is established by furnishing the correct answers at the end of each test.

You soon learn to recognize types of questions, forms of questions, and patterns of questioning. You may even begin to anticipate expected outcomes.

You perceive that many questions are repeated or adapted so that you can gain acute insights, which may enable you to score many sure points.

You learn how to confront new questions, or types of questions, and to attack them confidently and work out the correct answers.

You note objectives and emphases, and recognize pitfalls and dangers, so that you may make positive educational adjustments.

Moreover, you are kept fully informed in relation to new concepts, methods, practices, and directions in the field.

You discover that you are actually taking the examination all the time: you are preparing for the examination by "taking" an examination, not by reading extraneous and/or supererogatory textbooks.

In short, this PASSBOOK®, used directedly, should be an important factor in helping you to pass your test.

YOUTH GROUP SUPERVISOR

DUTIES:
Supervises assigned shifts of youth group workers in directing the activities of delinquent, dependent, or neglected children; is responsible and accountable for the security, custody and supervision of youthful offenders; assists in maintaining facility security and safety; performs related duties as required.

SUBJECT OF EXAMINATION:
The written test designed to evaluate knowledge, skills and /or abilities in the following areas:

1. **Child and adolescent development** - These questions test for knowledge and understanding of child and adolescent development. Questions may cover such topics as: concepts and principles of development; normal and abnormal patterns of behavior; dynamics of relationship formation; causes of problem behaviors; and the effects of peers, family, personality, and sociological influences on development and behavior.
2. **Situations and problems in supervising and counseling delinquent and/or socially-maladjusted youth** - These questions may cover such topics as: interviewing, counseling, supervising, and guiding youth with social adjustment problems; crisis intervention; handling emergencies; and working with staff, agencies, and families in supervising and guiding socially-maladjusted youth.
3. **Interviewing** - These questions test for knowledge of the principles and practices employed in obtaining information from individuals through structured conversations. These questions require you to apply the principles, practices, and techniques of effective interviewing to hypothetical interviewing situations. Included are questions that present a problem arising from an interviewing situation, and you must choose the most appropriate course of action to take.
4. **Supervision** - These questions test for knowledge of the principles and practices employed in planning, organizing, and controlling the activities of a work unit toward predetermined objectives. The concepts covered, usually in a situational question format, include such topics as assigning and reviewing work; evaluating performance; maintaining work standards; motivating and developing subordinates; implementing procedural change; increasing efficiency; and dealing with problems of absenteeism, morale, and discipline.
5. **Preparing written material** - These questions test for the ability to present information clearly and accurately, and to organize paragraphs logically and comprehensibly. For some questions, you will be given information in two or three sentences followed by four restatements of the information. You must then choose the best version. For other questions, you will be given paragraphs with their sentences out of order. You must then choose, from four suggestions, the best order for the sentences.

HOW TO TAKE A TEST

I. YOU MUST PASS AN EXAMINATION

A. *WHAT EVERY CANDIDATE SHOULD KNOW*

Examination applicants often ask us for help in preparing for the written test. What can I study in advance? What kinds of questions will be asked? How will the test be given? How will the papers be graded?

As an applicant for a civil service examination, you may be wondering about some of these things. Our purpose here is to suggest effective methods of advance study and to describe civil service examinations.

Your chances for success on this examination can be increased if you know how to prepare. Those "pre-examination jitters" can be reduced if you know what to expect. You can even experience an adventure in good citizenship if you know why civil service exams are given.

B. *WHY ARE CIVIL SERVICE EXAMINATIONS GIVEN?*

Civil service examinations are important to you in two ways. As a citizen, you want public jobs filled by employees who know how to do their work. As a job seeker, you want a fair chance to compete for that job on an equal footing with other candidates. The best-known means of accomplishing this two-fold goal is the competitive examination.

Exams are widely publicized throughout the nation. They may be administered for jobs in federal, state, city, municipal, town or village governments or agencies.

Any citizen may apply, with some limitations, such as the age or residence of applicants. Your experience and education may be reviewed to see whether you meet the requirements for the particular examination. When these requirements exist, they are reasonable and applied consistently to all applicants. Thus, a competitive examination may cause you some uneasiness now, but it is your privilege and safeguard.

C. *HOW ARE CIVIL SERVICE EXAMS DEVELOPED?*

Examinations are carefully written by trained technicians who are specialists in the field known as "psychological measurement," in consultation with recognized authorities in the field of work that the test will cover. These experts recommend the subject matter areas or skills to be tested; only those knowledges or skills important to your success on the job are included. The most reliable books and source materials available are used as references. Together, the experts and technicians judge the difficulty level of the questions.

Test technicians know how to phrase questions so that the problem is clearly stated. Their ethics do not permit "trick" or "catch" questions. Questions may have been tried out on sample groups, or subjected to statistical analysis, to determine their usefulness.

Written tests are often used in combination with performance tests, ratings of training and experience, and oral interviews. All of these measures combine to form the best-known means of finding the right person for the right job.

II. HOW TO PASS THE WRITTEN TEST

A. NATURE OF THE EXAMINATION

To prepare intelligently for civil service examinations, you should know how they differ from school examinations you have taken. In school you were assigned certain definite pages to read or subjects to cover. The examination questions were quite detailed and usually emphasized memory. Civil service exams, on the other hand, try to discover your present ability to perform the duties of a position, plus your potentiality to learn these duties. In other words, a civil service exam attempts to predict how successful you will be. Questions cover such a broad area that they cannot be as minute and detailed as school exam questions.

In the public service similar kinds of work, or positions, are grouped together in one "class." This process is known as *position-classification*. All the positions in a class are paid according to the salary range for that class. One class title covers all of these positions, and they are all tested by the same examination.

B. FOUR BASIC STEPS

1) Study the announcement

How, then, can you know what subjects to study? Our best answer is: "Learn as much as possible about the class of positions for which you've applied." The exam will test the knowledge, skills and abilities needed to do the work.

Your most valuable source of information about the position you want is the official exam announcement. This announcement lists the training and experience qualifications. Check these standards and apply only if you come reasonably close to meeting them.

The brief description of the position in the examination announcement offers some clues to the subjects which will be tested. Think about the job itself. Review the duties in your mind. Can you perform them, or are there some in which you are rusty? Fill in the blank spots in your preparation.

Many jurisdictions preview the written test in the exam announcement by including a section called "Knowledge and Abilities Required," "Scope of the Examination," or some similar heading. Here you will find out specifically what fields will be tested.

2) Review your own background

Once you learn in general what the position is all about, and what you need to know to do the work, ask yourself which subjects you already know fairly well and which need improvement. You may wonder whether to concentrate on improving your strong areas or on building some background in your fields of weakness. When the announcement has specified "some knowledge" or "considerable knowledge," or has used adjectives like "beginning principles of…" or "advanced … methods," you can get a clue as to the number and difficulty of questions to be asked in any given field. More questions, and hence broader coverage, would be included for those subjects which are more important in the work. Now weigh your strengths and weaknesses against the job requirements and prepare accordingly.

3) Determine the level of the position

Another way to tell how intensively you should prepare is to understand the level of the job for which you are applying. Is it the entering level? In other words, is this the position in which beginners in a field of work are hired? Or is it an intermediate or advanced level? Sometimes this is indicated by such words as "Junior" or "Senior" in the class title. Other jurisdictions use Roman numerals to designate the level – Clerk I, Clerk II, for example. The word "Supervisor" sometimes appears in the title. If the level is not indicated by the title, check the description of duties. Will you be working under very close supervision, or will you have responsibility for independent decisions in this work?

4) Choose appropriate study materials

Now that you know the subjects to be examined and the relative amount of each subject to be covered, you can choose suitable study materials. For beginning level jobs, or even advanced ones, if you have a pronounced weakness in some aspect of your training, read a modern, standard textbook in that field. Be sure it is up to date and has general coverage. Such books are normally available at your library, and the librarian will be glad to help you locate one. For entry-level positions, questions of appropriate difficulty are chosen – neither highly advanced questions, nor those too simple. Such questions require careful thought but not advanced training.

If the position for which you are applying is technical or advanced, you will read more advanced, specialized material. If you are already familiar with the basic principles of your field, elementary textbooks would waste your time. Concentrate on advanced textbooks and technical periodicals. Think through the concepts and review difficult problems in your field.

These are all general sources. You can get more ideas on your own initiative, following these leads. For example, training manuals and publications of the government agency which employs workers in your field can be useful, particularly for technical and professional positions. A letter or visit to the government department involved may result in more specific study suggestions, and certainly will provide you with a more definite idea of the exact nature of the position you are seeking.

III. KINDS OF TESTS

Tests are used for purposes other than measuring knowledge and ability to perform specified duties. For some positions, it is equally important to test ability to make adjustments to new situations or to profit from training. In others, basic mental abilities not dependent on information are essential. Questions which test these things may not appear as pertinent to the duties of the position as those which test for knowledge and information. Yet they are often highly important parts of a fair examination. For very general questions, it is almost impossible to help you direct your study efforts. What we can do is to point out some of the more common of these general abilities needed in public service positions and describe some typical questions.

1) General information

Broad, general information has been found useful for predicting job success in some kinds of work. This is tested in a variety of ways, from vocabulary lists to questions about current events. Basic background in some field of work, such as sociology or economics, may be sampled in a group of questions. Often these are principles which have become familiar to most persons through exposure rather than through formal training. It is difficult to advise you how to study for these questions; being alert to the world around you is our best suggestion.

2) Verbal ability

An example of an ability needed in many positions is verbal or language ability. Verbal ability is, in brief, the ability to use and understand words. Vocabulary and grammar tests are typical measures of this ability. Reading comprehension or paragraph interpretation questions are common in many kinds of civil service tests. You are given a paragraph of written material and asked to find its central meaning.

3) Numerical ability

Number skills can be tested by the familiar arithmetic problem, by checking paired lists of numbers to see which are alike and which are different, or by interpreting charts and graphs. In the latter test, a graph may be printed in the test booklet which you are asked to use as the basis for answering questions.

4) Observation

A popular test for law-enforcement positions is the observation test. A picture is shown to you for several minutes, then taken away. Questions about the picture test your ability to observe both details and larger elements.

5) Following directions

In many positions in the public service, the employee must be able to carry out written instructions dependably and accurately. You may be given a chart with several columns, each column listing a variety of information. The questions require you to carry out directions involving the information given in the chart.

6) Skills and aptitudes

Performance tests effectively measure some manual skills and aptitudes. When the skill is one in which you are trained, such as typing or shorthand, you can practice. These tests are often very much like those given in business school or high school courses. For many of the other skills and aptitudes, however, no short-time preparation can be made. Skills and abilities natural to you or that you have developed throughout your lifetime are being tested.

Many of the general questions just described provide all the data needed to answer the questions and ask you to use your reasoning ability to find the answers. Your best preparation for these tests, as well as for tests of facts and ideas, is to be at your physical and mental best. You, no doubt, have your own methods of getting into an exam-taking mood and keeping "in shape." The next section lists some ideas on this subject.

IV. KINDS OF QUESTIONS

Only rarely is the "essay" question, which you answer in narrative form, used in civil service tests. Civil service tests are usually of the short-answer type. Full instructions for answering these questions will be given to you at the examination. But in case this is your first experience with short-answer questions and separate answer sheets, here is what you need to know:

1) Multiple-choice Questions

Most popular of the short-answer questions is the "multiple choice" or "best answer" question. It can be used, for example, to test for factual knowledge, ability to solve problems or judgment in meeting situations found at work.

A multiple-choice question is normally one of three types—
- It can begin with an incomplete statement followed by several possible endings. You are to find the one ending which *best* completes the statement, although some of the others may not be entirely wrong.
- It can also be a complete statement in the form of a question which is answered by choosing one of the statements listed.

- It can be in the form of a problem – again you select the best answer.

Here is an example of a multiple-choice question with a discussion which should give you some clues as to the method for choosing the right answer:

When an employee has a complaint about his assignment, the action which will *best* help him overcome his difficulty is to
  A. discuss his difficulty with his coworkers
  B. take the problem to the head of the organization
  C. take the problem to the person who gave him the assignment
  D. say nothing to anyone about his complaint

In answering this question, you should study each of the choices to find which is best. Consider choice "A" – Certainly an employee may discuss his complaint with fellow employees, but no change or improvement can result, and the complaint remains unresolved. Choice "B" is a poor choice since the head of the organization probably does not know what assignment you have been given, and taking your problem to him is known as "going over the head" of the supervisor. The supervisor, or person who made the assignment, is the person who can clarify it or correct any injustice. Choice "C" is, therefore, correct. To say nothing, as in choice "D," is unwise. Supervisors have and interest in knowing the problems employees are facing, and the employee is seeking a solution to his problem.

2) True/False Questions

The "true/false" or "right/wrong" form of question is sometimes used. Here a complete statement is given. Your job is to decide whether the statement is right or wrong.

SAMPLE: A roaming cell-phone call to a nearby city costs less than a non-roaming call to a distant city.

This statement is wrong, or false, since roaming calls are more expensive.

This is not a complete list of all possible question forms, although most of the others are variations of these common types. You will always get complete directions for answering questions. Be sure you understand *how* to mark your answers – ask questions until you do.

V. RECORDING YOUR ANSWERS

Computer terminals are used more and more today for many different kinds of exams.

For an examination with very few applicants, you may be told to record your answers in the test booklet itself. Separate answer sheets are much more common. If this separate answer sheet is to be scored by machine – and this is often the case – it is highly important that you mark your answers correctly in order to get credit.

An electronic scoring machine is often used in civil service offices because of the speed with which papers can be scored. Machine-scored answer sheets must be marked with a pencil, which will be given to you. This pencil has a high graphite content which responds to the electronic scoring machine. As a matter of fact, stray dots may register as answers, so do not let your pencil rest on the answer sheet while you are pondering the correct answer. Also, if your pencil lead breaks or is otherwise defective, ask for another.

Since the answer sheet will be dropped in a slot in the scoring machine, be careful not to bend the corners or get the paper crumpled.

The answer sheet normally has five vertical columns of numbers, with 30 numbers to a column. These numbers correspond to the question numbers in your test booklet. After each number, going across the page are four or five pairs of dotted lines. These short dotted lines have small letters or numbers above them. The first two pairs may also have a "T" or "F" above the letters. This indicates that the first two pairs only are to be used if the questions are of the true-false type. If the questions are multiple choice, disregard the "T" and "F" and pay attention only to the small letters or numbers.

Answer your questions in the manner of the sample that follows:

32. The largest city in the United States is
    A. Washington, D.C.
    B. New York City
    C. Chicago
    D. Detroit
    E. San Francisco

1) Choose the answer you think is best. (New York City is the largest, so "B" is correct.)
2) Find the row of dotted lines numbered the same as the question you are answering. (Find row number 32)
3) Find the pair of dotted lines corresponding to the answer. (Find the pair of lines under the mark "B.")
4) Make a solid black mark between the dotted lines.

VI. BEFORE THE TEST

Common sense will help you find procedures to follow to get ready for an examination. Too many of us, however, overlook these sensible measures. Indeed, nervousness and fatigue have been found to be the most serious reasons why applicants fail to do their best on civil service tests. Here is a list of reminders:

- Begin your preparation early – Don't wait until the last minute to go scurrying around for books and materials or to find out what the position is all about.
- Prepare continuously – An hour a night for a week is better than an all-night cram session. This has been definitely established. What is more, a night a week for a month will return better dividends than crowding your study into a shorter period of time.
- Locate the place of the exam – You have been sent a notice telling you when and where to report for the examination. If the location is in a different town or otherwise unfamiliar to you, it would be well to inquire the best route and learn something about the building.
- Relax the night before the test – Allow your mind to rest. Do not study at all that night. Plan some mild recreation or diversion; then go to bed early and get a good night's sleep.
- Get up early enough to make a leisurely trip to the place for the test – This way unforeseen events, traffic snarls, unfamiliar buildings, etc. will not upset you.
- Dress comfortably – A written test is not a fashion show. You will be known by number and not by name, so wear something comfortable.

- Leave excess paraphernalia at home – Shopping bags and odd bundles will get in your way. You need bring only the items mentioned in the official notice you received; usually everything you need is provided. Do not bring reference books to the exam. They will only confuse those last minutes and be taken away from you when in the test room.
- Arrive somewhat ahead of time – If because of transportation schedules you must get there very early, bring a newspaper or magazine to take your mind off yourself while waiting.
- Locate the examination room – When you have found the proper room, you will be directed to the seat or part of the room where you will sit. Sometimes you are given a sheet of instructions to read while you are waiting. Do not fill out any forms until you are told to do so; just read them and be prepared.
- Relax and prepare to listen to the instructions
- If you have any physical problem that may keep you from doing your best, be sure to tell the test administrator. If you are sick or in poor health, you really cannot do your best on the exam. You can come back and take the test some other time.

VII. AT THE TEST

The day of the test is here and you have the test booklet in your hand. The temptation to get going is very strong. Caution! There is more to success than knowing the right answers. You must know how to identify your papers and understand variations in the type of short-answer question used in this particular examination. Follow these suggestions for maximum results from your efforts:

1) Cooperate with the monitor

The test administrator has a duty to create a situation in which you can be as much at ease as possible. He will give instructions, tell you when to begin, check to see that you are marking your answer sheet correctly, and so on. He is not there to guard you, although he will see that your competitors do not take unfair advantage. He wants to help you do your best.

2) Listen to all instructions

Don't jump the gun! Wait until you understand all directions. In most civil service tests you get more time than you need to answer the questions. So don't be in a hurry. Read each word of instructions until you clearly understand the meaning. Study the examples, listen to all announcements and follow directions. Ask questions if you do not understand what to do.

3) Identify your papers

Civil service exams are usually identified by number only. You will be assigned a number; you must not put your name on your test papers. Be sure to copy your number correctly. Since more than one exam may be given, copy your exact examination title.

4) Plan your time

Unless you are told that a test is a "speed" or "rate of work" test, speed itself is usually not important. Time enough to answer all the questions will be provided, but this does not mean that you have all day. An overall time limit has been set. Divide the total time (in minutes) by the number of questions to determine the approximate time you have for each question.

5) Do not linger over difficult questions

If you come across a difficult question, mark it with a paper clip (useful to have along) and come back to it when you have been through the booklet. One caution if you do this – be sure to skip a number on your answer sheet as well. Check often to be sure that you have not lost your place and that you are marking in the row numbered the same as the question you are answering.

6) Read the questions

Be sure you know what the question asks! Many capable people are unsuccessful because they failed to *read* the questions correctly.

7) Answer all questions

Unless you have been instructed that a penalty will be deducted for incorrect answers, it is better to guess than to omit a question.

8) Speed tests

It is often better NOT to guess on speed tests. It has been found that on timed tests people are tempted to spend the last few seconds before time is called in marking answers at random – without even reading them – in the hope of picking up a few extra points. To discourage this practice, the instructions may warn you that your score will be "corrected" for guessing. That is, a penalty will be applied. The incorrect answers will be deducted from the correct ones, or some other penalty formula will be used.

9) Review your answers

If you finish before time is called, go back to the questions you guessed or omitted to give them further thought. Review other answers if you have time.

10) Return your test materials

If you are ready to leave before others have finished or time is called, take ALL your materials to the monitor and leave quietly. Never take any test material with you. The monitor can discover whose papers are not complete, and taking a test booklet may be grounds for disqualification.

VIII. EXAMINATION TECHNIQUES

1) Read the general instructions carefully. These are usually printed on the first page of the exam booklet. As a rule, these instructions refer to the timing of the examination; the fact that you should not start work until the signal and must stop work at a signal, etc. If there are any *special* instructions, such as a choice of questions to be answered, make sure that you note this instruction carefully.

2) When you are ready to start work on the examination, that is as soon as the signal has been given, read the instructions to each question booklet, underline any key words or phrases, such as *least, best, outline, describe* and the like. In this way you will tend to answer as requested rather than discover on reviewing your paper that you *listed without describing*, that you selected the *worst* choice rather than the *best* choice, etc.

3) If the examination is of the objective or multiple-choice type – that is, each question will also give a series of possible answers: A, B, C or D, and you are called upon to select the best answer and write the letter next to that answer on your answer paper – it is advisable to start answering each question in turn. There may be anywhere from 50 to 100 such questions in the three or four hours allotted and you can see how much time would be taken if you read through all the questions before beginning to answer any. Furthermore, if you come across a question or group of questions which you know would be difficult to answer, it would undoubtedly affect your handling of all the other questions.

4) If the examination is of the essay type and contains but a few questions, it is a moot point as to whether you should read all the questions before starting to answer any one. Of course, if you are given a choice – say five out of seven and the like – then it is essential to read all the questions so you can eliminate the two that are most difficult. If, however, you are asked to answer all the questions, there may be danger in trying to answer the easiest one first because you may find that you will spend too much time on it. The best technique is to answer the first question, then proceed to the second, etc.

5) Time your answers. Before the exam begins, write down the time it started, then add the time allowed for the examination and write down the time it must be completed, then divide the time available somewhat as follows:
    - If 3-1/2 hours are allowed, that would be 210 minutes. If you have 80 objective-type questions, that would be an average of 2-1/2 minutes per question. Allow yourself no more than 2 minutes per question, or a total of 160 minutes, which will permit about 50 minutes to review.
    - If for the time allotment of 210 minutes there are 7 essay questions to answer, that would average about 30 minutes a question. Give yourself only 25 minutes per question so that you have about 35 minutes to review.

6) The most important instruction is to *read each question* and make sure you know what is wanted. The second most important instruction is to *time yourself properly* so that you answer every question. The third most important instruction is to *answer every question*. Guess if you have to but include something for each question. Remember that you will receive no credit for a blank and will probably receive some credit if you write something in answer to an essay question. If you guess a letter – say "B" for a multiple-choice question – you may have guessed right. If you leave a blank as an answer to a multiple-choice question, the examiners may respect your feelings but it will not add a point to your score. Some exams may penalize you for wrong answers, so in such cases *only*, you may not want to guess unless you have some basis for your answer.

7) Suggestions
    a. Objective-type questions
        1. Examine the question booklet for proper sequence of pages and questions
        2. Read all instructions carefully
        3. Skip any question which seems too difficult; return to it after all other questions have been answered
        4. Apportion your time properly; do not spend too much time on any single question or group of questions

5. Note and underline key words – *all, most, fewest, least, best, worst, same, opposite,* etc.
6. Pay particular attention to negatives
7. Note unusual option, e.g., unduly long, short, complex, different or similar in content to the body of the question
8. Observe the use of "hedging" words – *probably, may, most likely,* etc.
9. Make sure that your answer is put next to the same number as the question
10. Do not second-guess unless you have good reason to believe the second answer is definitely more correct
11. Cross out original answer if you decide another answer is more accurate; do not erase until you are ready to hand your paper in
12. Answer all questions; guess unless instructed otherwise
13. Leave time for review

  b. Essay questions
1. Read each question carefully
2. Determine exactly what is wanted. Underline key words or phrases.
3. Decide on outline or paragraph answer
4. Include many different points and elements unless asked to develop any one or two points or elements
5. Show impartiality by giving pros and cons unless directed to select one side only
6. Make and write down any assumptions you find necessary to answer the questions
7. Watch your English, grammar, punctuation and choice of words
8. Time your answers; don't crowd material

8) Answering the essay question

Most essay questions can be answered by framing the specific response around several key words or ideas. Here are a few such key words or ideas:

M's: manpower, materials, methods, money, management
P's: purpose, program, policy, plan, procedure, practice, problems, pitfalls, personnel, public relations

  a. Six basic steps in handling problems:
1. Preliminary plan and background development
2. Collect information, data and facts
3. Analyze and interpret information, data and facts
4. Analyze and develop solutions as well as make recommendations
5. Prepare report and sell recommendations
6. Install recommendations and follow up effectiveness

  b. Pitfalls to avoid
1. *Taking things for granted* – A statement of the situation does not necessarily imply that each of the elements is necessarily true; for example, a complaint may be invalid and biased so that all that can be taken for granted is that a complaint has been registered

2. *Considering only one side of a situation* – Wherever possible, indicate several alternatives and then point out the reasons you selected the best one
3. *Failing to indicate follow up* – Whenever your answer indicates action on your part, make certain that you will take proper follow-up action to see how successful your recommendations, procedures or actions turn out to be
4. *Taking too long in answering any single question* – Remember to time your answers properly

IX. AFTER THE TEST

Scoring procedures differ in detail among civil service jurisdictions although the general principles are the same. Whether the papers are hand-scored or graded by machine we have described, they are nearly always graded by number. That is, the person who marks the paper knows only the number – never the name – of the applicant. Not until all the papers have been graded will they be matched with names. If other tests, such as training and experience or oral interview ratings have been given, scores will be combined. Different parts of the examination usually have different weights. For example, the written test might count 60 percent of the final grade, and a rating of training and experience 40 percent. In many jurisdictions, veterans will have a certain number of points added to their grades.

After the final grade has been determined, the names are placed in grade order and an eligible list is established. There are various methods for resolving ties between those who get the same final grade – probably the most common is to place first the name of the person whose application was received first. Job offers are made from the eligible list in the order the names appear on it. You will be notified of your grade and your rank as soon as all these computations have been made. This will be done as rapidly as possible.

People who are found to meet the requirements in the announcement are called "eligibles." Their names are put on a list of eligible candidates. An eligible's chances of getting a job depend on how high he stands on this list and how fast agencies are filling jobs from the list.

When a job is to be filled from a list of eligibles, the agency asks for the names of people on the list of eligibles for that job. When the civil service commission receives this request, it sends to the agency the names of the three people highest on this list. Or, if the job to be filled has specialized requirements, the office sends the agency the names of the top three persons who meet these requirements from the general list.

The appointing officer makes a choice from among the three people whose names were sent to him. If the selected person accepts the appointment, the names of the others are put back on the list to be considered for future openings.

That is the rule in hiring from all kinds of eligible lists, whether they are for typist, carpenter, chemist, or something else. For every vacancy, the appointing officer has his choice of any one of the top three eligibles on the list. This explains why the person whose name is on top of the list sometimes does not get an appointment when some of the persons lower on the list do. If the appointing officer chooses the second or third eligible, the No. 1 eligible does not get a job at once, but stays on the list until he is appointed or the list is terminated.

X. HOW TO PASS THE INTERVIEW TEST

The examination for which you applied requires an oral interview test. You have already taken the written test and you are now being called for the interview test – the final part of the formal examination.

You may think that it is not possible to prepare for an interview test and that there are no procedures to follow during an interview. Our purpose is to point out some things you can do in advance that will help you and some good rules to follow and pitfalls to avoid while you are being interviewed.

What is an interview supposed to test?

The written examination is designed to test the technical knowledge and competence of the candidate; the oral is designed to evaluate intangible qualities, not readily measured otherwise, and to establish a list showing the relative fitness of each candidate – as measured against his competitors – for the position sought. Scoring is not on the basis of "right" and "wrong," but on a sliding scale of values ranging from "not passable" to "outstanding." As a matter of fact, it is possible to achieve a relatively low score without a single "incorrect" answer because of evident weakness in the qualities being measured.

Occasionally, an examination may consist entirely of an oral test – either an individual or a group oral. In such cases, information is sought concerning the technical knowledges and abilities of the candidate, since there has been no written examination for this purpose. More commonly, however, an oral test is used to supplement a written examination.

Who conducts interviews?

The composition of oral boards varies among different jurisdictions. In nearly all, a representative of the personnel department serves as chairman. One of the members of the board may be a representative of the department in which the candidate would work. In some cases, "outside experts" are used, and, frequently, a businessman or some other representative of the general public is asked to serve. Labor and management or other special groups may be represented. The aim is to secure the services of experts in the appropriate field.

However the board is composed, it is a good idea (and not at all improper or unethical) to ascertain in advance of the interview who the members are and what groups they represent. When you are introduced to them, you will have some idea of their backgrounds and interests, and at least you will not stutter and stammer over their names.

What should be done before the interview?

While knowledge about the board members is useful and takes some of the surprise element out of the interview, there is other preparation which is more substantive. It *is* possible to prepare for an oral interview – in several ways:

1) Keep a copy of your application and review it carefully before the interview

This may be the only document before the oral board, and the starting point of the interview. Know what education and experience you have listed there, and the sequence and dates of all of it. Sometimes the board will ask you to review the highlights of your experience for them; you should not have to hem and haw doing it.

2) Study the class specification and the examination announcement

Usually, the oral board has one or both of these to guide them. The qualities, characteristics or knowledges required by the position sought are stated in these documents. They offer valuable clues as to the nature of the oral interview. For example, if the job involves supervisory responsibilities, the announcement will usually indicate that knowledge of modern supervisory methods and the qualifications of the candidate as a supervisor will be tested. If so, you can expect such questions, frequently in the form of a hypothetical situation which you are expected to solve. NEVER go into an oral without knowledge of the duties and responsibilities of the job you seek.

3) Think through each qualification required

Try to visualize the kind of questions you would ask if you were a board member. How well could you answer them? Try especially to appraise your own knowledge and background in each area, *measured against the job sought*, and identify any areas in which you are weak. Be critical and realistic – do not flatter yourself.

4) Do some general reading in areas in which you feel you may be weak

For example, if the job involves supervision and your past experience has NOT, some general reading in supervisory methods and practices, particularly in the field of human relations, might be useful. Do NOT study agency procedures or detailed manuals. The oral board will be testing your understanding and capacity, not your memory.

5) Get a good night's sleep and watch your general health and mental attitude

You will want a clear head at the interview. Take care of a cold or any other minor ailment, and of course, no hangovers.

What should be done on the day of the interview?

Now comes the day of the interview itself. Give yourself plenty of time to get there. Plan to arrive somewhat ahead of the scheduled time, particularly if your appointment is in the fore part of the day. If a previous candidate fails to appear, the board might be ready for you a bit early. By early afternoon an oral board is almost invariably behind schedule if there are many candidates, and you may have to wait. Take along a book or magazine to read, or your application to review, but leave any extraneous material in the waiting room when you go in for your interview. In any event, relax and compose yourself.

The matter of dress is important. The board is forming impressions about you – from your experience, your manners, your attitude, and your appearance. Give your personal appearance careful attention. Dress your best, but not your flashiest. Choose conservative, appropriate clothing, and be sure it is immaculate. This is a business interview, and your appearance should indicate that you regard it as such. Besides, being well groomed and properly dressed will help boost your confidence.

Sooner or later, someone will call your name and escort you into the interview room. *This is it.* From here on you are on your own. It is too late for any more preparation. But remember, you asked for this opportunity to prove your fitness, and you are here because your request was granted.

What happens when you go in?

The usual sequence of events will be as follows: The clerk (who is often the board stenographer) will introduce you to the chairman of the oral board, who will introduce you to the other members of the board. Acknowledge the introductions before you sit down. Do not be surprised if you find a microphone facing you or a stenotypist sitting by. Oral interviews are usually recorded in the event of an appeal or other review.

Usually the chairman of the board will open the interview by reviewing the highlights of your education and work experience from your application – primarily for the benefit of the other members of the board, as well as to get the material into the record. Do not interrupt or comment unless there is an error or significant misinterpretation; if that is the case, do not hesitate. But do not quibble about insignificant matters. Also, he will usually ask you some question about your education, experience or your present job – partly to get you to start talking and to establish the interviewing "rapport." He may start the actual questioning, or turn it over to one of the other members. Frequently, each member undertakes the questioning on a particular area, one in which he is perhaps most competent, so you can expect each member to participate in the examination. Because time is limited, you may also expect some rather abrupt switches in the direction the questioning takes, so do not be upset by it. Normally, a board member will not pursue a single line of questioning unless he discovers a particular strength or weakness.

After each member has participated, the chairman will usually ask whether any member has any further questions, then will ask you if you have anything you wish to add. Unless you are expecting this question, it may floor you. Worse, it may start you off on an extended, extemporaneous speech. The board is not usually seeking more information. The question is principally to offer you a last opportunity to present further qualifications or to indicate that you have nothing to add. So, if you feel that a significant qualification or characteristic has been overlooked, it is proper to point it out in a sentence or so. Do not compliment the board on the thoroughness of their examination – they have been sketchy, and you know it. If you wish, merely say, "No thank you, I have nothing further to add." This is a point where you can "talk yourself out" of a good impression or fail to present an important bit of information. Remember, *you close the interview yourself*.

The chairman will then say, "That is all, Mr. _____, thank you." Do not be startled; the interview is over, and quicker than you think. Thank him, gather your belongings and take your leave. Save your sigh of relief for the other side of the door.

How to put your best foot forward

Throughout this entire process, you may feel that the board individually and collectively is trying to pierce your defenses, seek out your hidden weaknesses and embarrass and confuse you. Actually, this is not true. They are obliged to make an appraisal of your qualifications for the job you are seeking, and they want to see you in your best light. Remember, they must interview all candidates and a non-cooperative candidate may become a failure in spite of their best efforts to bring out his qualifications. Here are 15 suggestions that will help you:

1) Be natural – Keep your attitude confident, not cocky

If you are not confident that you can do the job, do not expect the board to be. Do not apologize for your weaknesses, try to bring out your strong points. The board is interested in a positive, not negative, presentation. Cockiness will antagonize any board member and make him wonder if you are covering up a weakness by a false show of strength.

2) Get comfortable, but don't lounge or sprawl

Sit erectly but not stiffly. A careless posture may lead the board to conclude that you are careless in other things, or at least that you are not impressed by the importance of the occasion. Either conclusion is natural, even if incorrect. Do not fuss with your clothing, a pencil or an ashtray. Your hands may occasionally be useful to emphasize a point; do not let them become a point of distraction.

3) Do not wisecrack or make small talk

This is a serious situation, and your attitude should show that you consider it as such. Further, the time of the board is limited – they do not want to waste it, and neither should you.

4) Do not exaggerate your experience or abilities

In the first place, from information in the application or other interviews and sources, the board may know more about you than you think. Secondly, you probably will not get away with it. An experienced board is rather adept at spotting such a situation, so do not take the chance.

5) If you know a board member, do not make a point of it, yet do not hide it

Certainly you are not fooling him, and probably not the other members of the board. Do not try to take advantage of your acquaintanceship – it will probably do you little good.

6) Do not dominate the interview

Let the board do that. They will give you the clues – do not assume that you have to do all the talking. Realize that the board has a number of questions to ask you, and do not try to take up all the interview time by showing off your extensive knowledge of the answer to the first one.

7) Be attentive

You only have 20 minutes or so, and you should keep your attention at its sharpest throughout. When a member is addressing a problem or question to you, give him your undivided attention. Address your reply principally to him, but do not exclude the other board members.

8) Do not interrupt

A board member may be stating a problem for you to analyze. He will ask you a question when the time comes. Let him state the problem, and wait for the question.

9) Make sure you understand the question

Do not try to answer until you are sure what the question is. If it is not clear, restate it in your own words or ask the board member to clarify it for you. However, do not haggle about minor elements.

10) Reply promptly but not hastily

A common entry on oral board rating sheets is "candidate responded readily," or "candidate hesitated in replies." Respond as promptly and quickly as you can, but do not jump to a hasty, ill-considered answer.

11) Do not be peremptory in your answers

A brief answer is proper – but do not fire your answer back. That is a losing game from your point of view. The board member can probably ask questions much faster than you can answer them.

12) Do not try to create the answer you think the board member wants

He is interested in what kind of mind you have and how it works – not in playing games. Furthermore, he can usually spot this practice and will actually grade you down on it.

13) Do not switch sides in your reply merely to agree with a board member

Frequently, a member will take a contrary position merely to draw you out and to see if you are willing and able to defend your point of view. Do not start a debate, yet do not surrender a good position. If a position is worth taking, it is worth defending.

14) Do not be afraid to admit an error in judgment if you are shown to be wrong
The board knows that you are forced to reply without any opportunity for careful consideration. Your answer may be demonstrably wrong. If so, admit it and get on with the interview.

15) Do not dwell at length on your present job
The opening question may relate to your present assignment. Answer the question but do not go into an extended discussion. You are being examined for a *new* job, not your present one. As a matter of fact, try to phrase ALL your answers in terms of the job for which you are being examined.

Basis of Rating
Probably you will forget most of these "do's" and "don'ts" when you walk into the oral interview room. Even remembering them all will not ensure you a passing grade. Perhaps you did not have the qualifications in the first place. But remembering them will help you to put your best foot forward, without treading on the toes of the board members.

Rumor and popular opinion to the contrary notwithstanding, an oral board wants you to make the best appearance possible. They know you are under pressure – but they also want to see how you respond to it as a guide to what your reaction would be under the pressures of the job you seek. They will be influenced by the degree of poise you display, the personal traits you show and the manner in which you respond.

ABOUT THIS BOOK

This book contains tests divided into Examination Sections. Go through each test, answering every question in the margin. We have also attached a sample answer sheet at the back of the book that can be removed and used. At the end of each test look at the answer key and check your answers. On the ones you got wrong, look at the right answer choice and learn. Do not fill in the answers first. Do not memorize the questions and answers, but understand the answer and principles involved. On your test, the questions will likely be different from the samples. Questions are changed and new ones added. If you understand these past questions you should have success with any changes that arise. Tests may consist of several types of questions. We have additional books on each subject should more study be advisable or necessary for you. Finally, the more you study, the better prepared you will be. This book is intended to be the last thing you study before you walk into the examination room. Prior study of relevant texts is also recommended. NLC publishes some of these in our Fundamental Series. Knowledge and good sense are important factors in passing your exam. Good luck also helps. So now study this Passbook, absorb the material contained within and take that knowledge into the examination. Then do your best to pass that exam.

EXAMINATION SECTION

EXAMINATION SECTION
TEST 1

DIRECTIONS: Each question or incomplete statement is followed by several suggested answers or completions. Select the one that BEST answers the question or completes the statement. *PRINT THE LETTER OF THE CORRECT ANSWER IN THE SPACE AT THE RIGHT.*

1. In working with adolescent groups, an important point to remember is to give

    A. guidance without taking matters out of the group's hands
    B. guidance to the youth leaders only
    C. assistance only when the groups ask for it
    D. direct assistance at every opportunity

2. The BASIC purpose to be kept in mind when programming group activities for delinquent adolescents is that

    A. group activities are natural for delinquents
    B. the activities should focus on control and discipline
    C. the youths should share in the program expenses
    D. the activities should focus on total freedom of expression

3. Workers assigned to your unit are experiencing difficulties with programming group activities. The programs seen to be out of context with the problems of the youths, and the youths are reported to be bored, evasive, and non-participating.
An important factor in programming that you, as unit supervisor, must teach them is

    A. to involve the group members in the planning and implementation of all programs
    B. to include current procedures like enounter, reality therapy, and crisis intervention
    C. that they must have individual meetings with key members to enlist their aid and assistance
    D. that they are not providing enough direction and control to the group meetings

4. The one of the following groups of characteristics which MOST correctly describes anti-social adolescent groups is

    A. fraternity, mutual respect, and interest in each other
    B. group loyalty, need to retaliate, and the necessity to fight
    C. divisiveness, mistrust, and self-centeredness
    D. none of the above

5. You are supervising a new worker who tells you, during his supervisory conference, that he feels that he has not been able to help his group to re-direct their energies into productive channels.
It would be BEST for you to advise this worker that

    A. he should not be discouraged because adolescents have boundless energy that is difficult to control
    B. adolescent groups respond to planning and direction, and that he should set up some simple form of organization
    C. the conflict and competition concept of group behavior requires group psychotherapy
    D. his anxieties are getting in the way of effective work with his group

6. A new worker in the unit under your supervision shows in his recording that he has been able to overcome his feelings of insecurity in his new role of working with his group and to work through the initial testing period imposed on him by the group. However, during his supervisory conference, you discover that he is extremely anxious because the group does not seem to be verbalizing their problems with him.
   You should advise this worker in conference that

   A. these are hard-core youths who do not talk about their problems
   B. his recording is weak, and should be done in process style for the next six months
   C. his anxiety is probably being communicated to the group, inhibiting them from verbalizing their problems
   D. a marathon encounter with the group may help them to verbalize their problems

7. In preparation for a staff conference covering principles of working with alienated youth groups, you assign different aspects of the subject to different workers. In his notes, the worker who is to discuss *process in working with groups* lists the following:
   1. sensitivity to the pace of group movement
   2. resistance and resentment arising from domination by the worker
   3. time and place of meetings
   An IMPORTANT part that was omitted by the worker is

   A. realistic programming
   B. awareness of *where the group is at*
   C. the importance of sensitivity training
   D. supervision

8. A youth worker reports to you in a supervisory conference that the youths in his group are unfriendly and bossy with each other, but that when he leaves them, roughhousing breaks out.
   The MOST likely explanation for this is that

   A. he is not exercising enough control
   B. he is probably too strict and tight with them
   C. this particular group of kids usually acts this way
   D. this is unusual behavior of alienated youth

9. The SIGNIFICANT factors that would distinguish a constructive and orderly group of adolescents from an anti-social gang are the

   A. aims, quality of the relationships, and behavior of the individuals
   B. aims, personality of the members, and locale
   C. age, problems, and behavior of the members
   D. locale, personality of the members, and leadership

10. Youth workers involved with groups of adolescent girls may have to deal with problems of sexual acting-out. Programming for girls involved in sexual acting-out should have as its BASIC purpose

    A. security building and developing a feeling of being needed and wanted
    B. sex information and a discussion of birth control and abortion
    C. rap sessions on dating, making out, and male-female psychology
    D. parties, dances, outings, and bus rides

11. Adolescents have many fears that they are ashamed to show because they are afraid of disapproval. Restraining these fears may lead to anxieties that could be even more troublesome.
    To help youths resolve such problems, youth service units should emphasize in their programming

    A. activities that help youths gain self-confidence
    B. rap sessions on anxiety
    C. activities that are not likely to produce fear
    D. hiking, swimming, wrestling, and basketball

12. All of the following are purposes of group counseling EXCEPT

    A. avoidance of treating pathology as such
    B. helping clients attain a better level of functioning
    C. modifying social and familial problems
    D. resolving intra-psychic conflicts

13. A MAJOR advantage of having group programs for local teenagers in Youth Services Agency neighborhood offices is that

    A. these programs are less expensive to operate
    B. the participating groups are mutual groups in their own environment
    C. this activity is necessary for suppressing riots
    D. such programs serve as good public relations

14. A worker reports about his youth council that one of the sub-groups in the council revolves around a boy who has many constructive ideas. However, this boy's participation is limited due to the rivalry between him and the elected president.
    The supervisor should advise the worker to

    A. have the leader of the sub-group excluded from the council
    B. help the leader of the sub-group participate more actively
    C. tell the leader of the sub-group to *play ball* with the rest of the council
    D. let the council settle this problem without outside assistance

15. One of your youth workers is having difficulty forming a group in a particular neighborhood. Parents in that area are upset about the idea of teenage groups. This worker plans to meet with some of these parents, and he asks your help in reaching a goal with them. As supervisor, you should advise him to approach this problem by

    A. helping the parents to see that group activities are a sign of a youth's growth, not of a lack of gratitude or affection for his parents
    B. informing the parents that it is the professional opinion of the Youth Services Agency that groups are necessary in order to serve youth constructively
    C. postponing this meeting until you can convince individual parents of the value of groups
    D. helping the parents to see that many of their teenagers are having difficulties at home and in school because they do not participate in group activities

16. Experts have described festivals, fairs, holidays, etc. as *nothing less nor more than excesses provided by law and which owe their cheerful character to the release which they bring.*
    The significance of this in programming unit projects is to

    A. have the workers assist the community in sponsoring fairs, block dances, etc.
    B. leave the sponsoring of fairs, dances, etc. to associations affiliated with the police department
    C. avoid involving large groups of people in public affairs because of the danger of fights, riots, etc.
    D. use a good part of the unit's budget for fairs, dances, bazaars, etc.

17. Which one of the groups listed below has the following four characteristics:
    1. Basic depressive character
    2. Intolerance for frustration and pain
    3. Lack of meaningful objects
    4. Artificial technique to maintain self-regard?

    A. College students
    B. Drug abusers
    C. Adolescents
    D. Alienated youth

18. The MOST important consideration in evaluating the ego strength of an angry, deprived, mistreated, frustrated, evasive client is the client's ability to

    A. verbalize his problems
    B. redirect his anger
    C. form a relationship with an accepting worker
    D. hold a job

19. When a worker, in his first interview with a parent, tries to take down a developmental history of a boy, he usually gets many meaningless answers, such as *It was normal* or *I don't remember.*
    The worker should realize that

    A. this information is inaccurate and should be disregarded
    B. the parent is under stress at first, and should be able to give more factual information later
    C. the parent purposely is withholding valuable information about the boy
    D. the parent must be told that if he cannot cooperate he cannot be helped

20. One of the workers under your supervision is puzzled as to why a mother she was working with broke off contacts prematurely. When you read the record of this mother, you learn that she had become overdependent upon the worker before suddenly stopping her visits.
    In the supervisory conference, you should help the worker to understand that this type of client

    A. is flighty, evasive, and has low reality testing
    B. is in need of deep psychotherapy
    C. is defending herself against this overdependence
    D. needs the chance to test her limits with an accepting person

21. When a worker is troubled because youths in his group ask him personal questions and he does not know how to answer them, as unit supervisor it would be BEST for you to advise the worker to

    A. interrogate the youths in detail about the reasons behind the questions
    B. tell the youths all they want to know, so that the worker appears friendly and human
    C. give a frank, brief, truthful answer and then immediately redirect the youths back to their own problems
    D. point out to the youths that the worker's personal life is not their business

22. Psychiatrists are usually concerned with the total functioning and integration of the human personality. Caseworkers usually concentrate on

    A. the same thing, but for shorter periods of time
    B. the same thing, but without prescribing medication
    C. helping the client to deal with the presenting problem
    D. all of the above

23. Some people feel that by cutting down temptations and stimuli, delinquency can be substantially decreased. Specific measures are curfews, eliminating the cruder forms of violence from the mass media, reducing the number of sexually stimulating publications available to youth, keeping down teenagers' resources for obtaining liquor, increasing recreational facilities, etc. The STRONGEST flaw in this approach is that

    A. it is not fair to non-delinquents
    B. it would not seriously affect the hard-core delinquent
    C. the community is not yet prepared for it
    D. it needs more time to prove itself

24. A COMMON error made by youth workers who are beginning to find out about the influence of unconscious desires and emotions on human behavior is to

    A. probe the client unnecessarily
    B. become over-assured that they can solve the client's problem
    C. slow up the pace of the interview
    D. look for the proper treatment method based on the client's neurosis

25. A basic technique which is used to obtain knowledge of the problem to be solved and sufficient understanding of the troubled person and of the situation, so that the problem can be solved effectively, is known as

    A. psychosomatics
    B. interviewing
    C. recording
    D. supervisory conferences

26. Which of the following is a CORRECT definition of the term *acceptance* as used in social work?

    A. A decision made at intake to accept the client as a case for the agency to handle
    B. The concept that the worker does not pass judgment on the client's behavior
    C. The concept of a positive and active understanding by the worker of the feelings a client expresses through his behavior
    D. Communication to the client that the worker does not condone and accept his anti-social behavior

27. Beginning youth workers are usually informed in a training session that they should be non-judgmental, should not become dependent on the client's liking them, and should not become angry. However, in an attempt to suppress these feelings, workers often behave in a stilted and artificial manner with clients.
As a supervisor, you should help your workers

    A. seek counseling to help them understand their angry feelings
    B. realize that they were not yet ready for that type of training
    C. understand that this artificiality will soon pass by as easily as it came
    D. recognize the naturalness of these feelings and learn to control their expression

28. A worker in the unit under your supervision has a youth in his group who has developed a strong antagonism toward him. You can find nothing that the worker has done to arouse such antagonism in the youth.
This antagonism is probably due to

    A. restrictions imposed on the client by the agency
    B. factors deeply hidden in the client's personality
    C. the youth's feeling of guilt because he has withheld information from the worker
    D. the fact that the worker may have promised the youth too much

29. The development of an emotional rapport, positive or negative, between the client and the worker is not abnormal, but inevitable. Sometimes the feelings that develop as a result of this rapport become excessively intense.
In those instances, the worker should

    A. request that the client be given another worker
    B. control the nature and intensity of the feelings
    C. ignore the feelings, which will disappear soon
    D. confront the client with the inappropriateness of these feelings

30. In social work, when we talk of ambivalence, we mean that the

    A. social worker refrains from imposing his moral judgments on the client
    B. supervisor assists the worker in understanding the psychological causes for client's behavior
    C. client has conflicting interests, desires, and emotions
    D. client is seeking someone who will understand the subjective reasons for his behavior

31. Although we can judge statements about objectively verifiable matters to be true or false, we are not similarly justified in passing judgments on subjective attitudes. This statement BEST explains the rationale behind the social work principle of

    A. empathy   B. self-awareness
    C. non-judgmentality   D. confidentiality

32. A psychological factor that explains why generally lawabiding individuals can become a part of a violent crowd is

    A. the deep urge for destruction and violence inherent in man
    B. the anonymity of the group would allow individuals to yield to restrained instincts
    C. that there is force in numbers, decreasing the likelihood of personal injury
    D. that man is basically a *herd animal,* so the mob is our natural environment

33. When you have learned that one of your workers has organized a protest, you should advise him to 33._____

    A. be aware that the group may not be able to defend themselves against the police
    B. alert the community to distract the police to another area
    C. call off the protest because of the probability of danger
    D. take precautions with his group in order to be sure that the protest will be orderly

34. Some local merchants are disturbed because they feel that a group of boys who *hang on the corner* will develop into a delinquent gang. They invite you, the unit supervisor, to address them at a meeting in order to describe the characteristics of delinquent gangs to them. 34._____
    In your talk to these merchants, you should

    A. describe how delinquent gangs make a career of hanging around, have a blind loyalty among members, and see destruction as their way of hitting back at society
    B. advise them to call off the meeting because the delinquent gang as such has disappeared
    C. assure them that they should not be concerned because you have a worker in that area who has this group under surveillance
    D. contact your area administrator because this involves a relationship with the community that is not on your level of responsibility

35. According to the REPORT OF THE NATIONAL ADVISORY COMMITTEE ON CIVIL DISORDERS, riots are dramatic forms of protest expressing 35._____

    A. hostility to government or private institutions
    B. undefined but real frustrations
    C. anger at the failure of society to provide certain groups with adequate opportunities
    D. all of the above

36. Many neighborhoods seem to develop a subculture in which forms of criminal and delinquent behavior and values are accepted as norms. 36._____
    If the unit area happens to be in one of these neighborhoods, the unit supervisor would be BEST advised to keep in mind that

    A. we know less about changing subcultures than we know about influencing groups and individuals
    B. it is easier to change subcultures than to influence groups and individuals
    C. subcultures are simple to identify, and helping the members to resolve their problems is comparatively easy
    D. this is only a theory and, therefore, should not influence the functioning of the unit office

37. The neighborhood drug abuse prevention network of the Addiction Services Agency is a series of broad-based community groups called 37._____

    A. CARE AND AWARE   B. EVIL AND WEAK
    C. RARE AND AWARE   D. NACE AND CARE

38. An agency whose sole purpose is to fight addiction through a comprehensive prevention and rehabilitation program is

   A. Daytop Village
   B. Narcotics Addiction Control Commission
   C. Addiction Services Agency
   D. Phoenix House

38.____

39. Agencies which have been traditionally used by the Youth Services Agency for the purpose of sponsoring approved group programs to help youth improve their behavior are:

   A. Madison-Felicia, Vocational Advisory Service, Catholic Youth Organization, United Neighborhood Houses, Federation Employment and Guidance Service, Community Centers
   B. Office of Economic Opportunity, Catholic Youth Organization, Police Athletic League, Federation Employment and Guidance Service, Vocational Advisory Service, Jewish Family Service, Federation of Protestant Welfare Agencies
   C. Catholic Youth Organization, United Neighborhood Houses, Young Men's Christian Association, Protestant Council, Police Athletic League, Builders For the Family and Youth
   D. Catholic Youth Organization, Young Men's Christian Association, Protestant Council, Police Athletic League, Office of Economic Opportunity, Builders For Family and Youth, Vocational Advisory Service

39.____

40. Agencies that are used by Youth Services Agency to provide individual casework treatment services for Youth Services Agency clients who need individual therapy for deep-seated problems are:

   A. Jewish Family Services, State Division for Youth, Catholic Charities, Staten Island Family Service, Salvation Army, Community Education
   B. Big Brothers, Catholic Charities, Jewish Board of Guardians, Jewish Family Services, Salvation Army
   C. Catholic Youth Organization, Vocational Advisory Service, Melrose Center, Federation Employment and Guidance Service, United Neighborhood Houses
   D. Catholic Charities, Jewish Family Service, Vocational Foundation, Vermont Program, Big Brothers, Boys' Harbor, Salvation Army

40.____

41. The Departments that make up the Human Resources Administration are:

   A. Manpower and Career Development, Office of Economic Opportunity, Commission on Civil Disorders, Youth Services Agency, Addiction Services, Social Services, Community Development
   B. Manpower and Career Development Agency, Office of Economic Opportunity, Youth Services Agency, Addiction Services Agency, Department of Social Services, Commission on Human Rights, Community Volunteers
   C. Human Resources Administration Central Staff, Man power and Career Development Agency, Community Development Agency, Department of Social Services, Youth Services Agency, Addiction Services Agency, Office of Education Affairs
   D. Human Resources Administration Central Staff, Manpower and Career Development Agency, Department of Social Services, Youth Services Agency, Addiction Services Agency, Office of Economic Opportunity, Commission on Human Rights

41.____

42. A Youth Services Agency project that was developed in 1968 in response to the findings of the National Advisory Commission on Civil Disorders (Kerner-Lindsay Report) and which was designed to develop and demonstrate model approaches to engender interracial understanding between teenagers is the 42._____

    A. Youth Opportunity Center
    B. Demonstration and Training Unit
    C. Interdepartmental Neighborhood Service Center
    D. Vermont Project

43. Which one of the following is mandated to provide services to the poverty-stricken, to improve the quality of these services and the methods of delivering them, to carry out the legal commitment to the poor, and to help the poor to help themselves? 43._____

    A. Office of Economic Opportunity
    B. Environmental Resources Administration
    C. Community Action Program
    D. Model Cities Program

44. An indication of mature behavior to be sought for in the client and encouraged by the youth worker is the 44._____

    A. ability to become involved in issues of racism, urban life, and human rights
    B. development of some controls over the impulse to act out
    C. formulation of definite and specific goals in careers
    D. steady, consistent pattern of behavior that is relatively free of ambivalent feelings

45. That point in human development which marks a person's passage into adolescence is known as 45._____

    A. maturity   B. the Oedipal stage
    C. the genital stage   D. puberty

46. An important factor to remember about the mental, physical, social, and emotional growth of an adolescent is that the 46._____

    A. pace is uneven and individual
    B. pace is relatively even
    C. rate of growth is predictable
    D. growth has no special pattern

47. Adolescents are more likely to understand the concrete and the specific, rather than general ideas like justice, honesty, love, etc. 47._____
    The implication of this concept for the unit supervisor in guiding his staff is

    A. that programming should include recreation, job counseling, school help, and visits at times of crisis
    B. the necessity to make sure that the programs use a large part of their budget for *treats* for the youth
    C. to be sure the staff is directing much of their energy into pointing up the importance of these general concepts
    D. to help the youths understand that life has taught them to be mistrustful

48. The theory of juvenile delinquency that traces much of delinquency back to failures in family relationships during the early years of childhood, and to continuing family difficulties, offers help to the youth worker in

    A. forming a general picture of the typical delinquent
    B. understanding that fighting is one of the best ways to rise to the top
    C. identifying normal growth needs of adolescents and the obstacles against healthy maturity
    D. realizing that delinquents are children at heart and are best treated as children

49. The theory of juvenile delinquency which holds that youths from minority groups turn to anti-social behavior when they feel that their access to social, educational, and economic opportunities in legal and approved ways is blocked has had a strong impact on the establishment of agencies like the

    A. Job Corps
    B. Community Development Agency
    C. Youth Board of the 1950's
    D. Addiction Services Agency

50. Which of the following is a descriptive term for a client who is resistive, breaks appointments, withholds information, beclouds issues, relates to others in a primitive, often distorted, fashion, and acts out his wishes and conflicts in his contact with the worker?

    A. Psychotic
    B. Narcotics addict
    C. Schizophrenic
    D. Character disorder

KEY (CORRECT ANSWERS)

1. A	11. A	21. C	31. C	41. C
2. B	12. D	22. C	32. B	42. D
3. A	13. B	23. B	33. D	43. A
4. B	14. B	24. A	34. A	44. B
5. B	15. A	25. B	35. D	45. D
6. C	16. A	26. C	36. A	46. A
7. A	17. B	27. D	37. C	47. A
8. B	18. C	28. B	38. C	48. C
9. A	19. B	29. B	39. C	49. A
10. A	20. C	30. C	40. B	50. D

TEST 2

DIRECTIONS: Each question or incomplete statement is followed by several suggested answers or completions. Select the one that BEST answers the question or completes the statement. *PRINT THE LETTER OF THE CORRECT ANSWER IN THE SPACE AT THE RIGHT.*

1. Adolescents who become involved in delinquent behavior are usually angry or frustrated a large part of their time. Conscious awareness of the intensity of their needs makes them feel weak.
   For this reason, they frequently

   A. are easier to work with
   B. prefer strong male youth workers
   C. need to be controlled and disciplined
   D. have to show the world they don't care what happens

   1.____

2. Sociologists and behavioral scientists provided the ideas of cohesion, conflict, competition, cooperation, authority, leadership, and stratification that are clearly manifested in

   A. supervision
   B. addiction
   C. group behavior
   D. casework therapy

   2.____

3. The one of the following causes of juvenile delinquency among sub-lower class youth which has been given increased attention in recent years is the

   A. prevalence of the one-parent family
   B. failure of family relationships in the early years
   C. blockage of educational, vocational, and social opportunities
   D. emotional problems and psychiatric disorders of youth

   3.____

4. A high-ranking official recently stated that some youths have made suicide attempts in detention centers so that they would be transferred from the detention centers to hospitals.
   If the workers in a unit should bring this topic up for discussion in a staff meeting, the supervisor should

   A. instruct workers to inform the youths of the area about this method of getting out of a detention center
   B. have a worker visit a youth in detention in order to observe and report back to the unit so that a demonstration can be organized
   C. assign different workers to study various aspects of the problem in order to plan an intelligent, informed discussion
   D. point out that the worker does not directly become involved with this problem, and direct the discussion to a more pertinent topic

   4.____

5. The MOST significant characteristics of the daily lives of alienated youths can be described as

   A. their days are aimless, disorganized, and unproductive
   B. they spend most of their time in antisocial activity
   C. they spend a good portion of their time seeking a means of earning money
   D. they concentrate most of their energies on actingout

   5.____

6. A young man drops into the office to request help in finding a job. While he is waiting to see the office coverage worker, you notice he is nervous, sweating, yawning, and constantly blowing his nose.
   As a unit supervisor, you should

   A. overlook this because the youth is probably worried about getting a job, and is dirty and tired
   B. feel assured that the worker will observe this also and handle it in the best possible way
   C. advise the worker of your observations, and discuss the possible causes of this behavior with the worker
   D. do none of the above

7. The *battered child syndrome* is reported to be one of the most difficult problems facing health officials.
   When a worker knows of a case of a boy being severely abused physically by his parents, the supervisor should advise the worker to

   A. discuss this with a psychiatrist to find out why the parent is abusing the child
   B. tell the child to stay away from the parents as much as possible
   C. try to talk to the parents to help them see what they are doing wrong
   D. report the situation to the Bureau of Child Welfare of the Department of Social Services

8. Ghetto youth today present symptoms of delinquent behavior that are in many ways more disruptive than those of the anti-social gang members of the 1950's. Some of these symptoms are

   A. alienation, school drop-outs, drug addiction, loosely formed cliques
   B. interracial conflicts, community violence, few family ties, teenage drifters, and panhandlers
   C. promiscuity, alcoholism, vandalism, homosexuality, venereal disease
   D. all of the above

9. A psychological factor that tends to make the spread of drug abuse today easier among siblings in a family is the

   A. necessity for drug users to seduce others to join them
   B. need of siblings to rebel against parents
   C. fact that siblings can more easily *cover* for each other
   D. fact that older siblings can force younger siblings to take drugs

10. A parent complains to a worker that her teenage son is hanging around with a *bad bunch,* that money is strangely missing from the house lately, that his eating habits have changed, and that he spends long periods of time alone.
    When the worker discusses this with the unit supervisor, the supervisor should

    A. interview the parent as soon as possible to get more precise information
    B. advise the worker to refer the parent to a doctor to have her son examined
    C. help the worker to be supportive to the parent and try to make contact with the son
    D. assure him the parent is just jumpy over the drug scare and there is probably another explanation for the boy's behavior

11. A worker reports that the youths in his area think that *blowing pot* is all right because marijuana is not addictive, is harmless in small doses, and is far less dangerous than alcohol. The worker asks your help to talk the kids out of *blowing pot.*
    You, as unit supervisor, should

    A. advise the worker to refer the youths to the nearest, best drug rehabilitation resource
    B. give the worker enough literature so the youths could learn more about the situation
    C. assure the worker that these facts are true
    D. help the worker to involve the youths in constructive group activities

11.____

12. It is important for the youth worker to understand that the adolescent's FIRST loyalty belongs to his

    A. peer group   B. siblings
    C. parents   D. best friend

12.____

13. One of the workers in a unit office reports that he is having some difficulty with his group of youths. It is apparent that the youth leader of the group is seriously disturbed.
    The BEST action for the worker to take FIRST is to

    A. try to redirect the leader's activities into more constructive channels
    B. help the group select a leader who is more psychologically sound
    C. take steps to have the leader removed from the community into a setting where he can get psychiatric help
    D. show this leader where his behavior is hurting the group so that he can change his behavior

13.____

14. The pleasurable effect produced by heroin is the

    A. feeling of excitement and energy
    B. expansion of sense perceptions
    C. feeling of relaxation, sociability, and good humor
    D. suppression of fears, tensions, and anxieties

14.____

15. The many rumors that spread throughout the Youth Services Agency are harmful to the morale of the staff because they result in worry, suspicion, mistrust, and uncertainty. The BEST way the unit supervisor can stop a rumor is to

    A. disregard it
    B. deny it
    C. start a different one
    D. give the staff the true facts

15.____

16. Parental rejection and neglect damage the personality of the developing child, and orient the child toward his agemates in the neighborhood.
    This statement would BEST describe the mechanism that leads to

    A. delinquency in urban industrial areas
    B. the establishment of neighborhood clubs
    C. the generation gap
    D. drug addiction

16.____

17. Many young people are introduced to drugs by friends. Youths don't like to be called *chicken,* they like to be *hip* like the rest, and they have to be a part of something. When a worker asks for your guidance on handling one of his youths who is being pressured into getting *high* by his friends, as the unit supervisor, you should help the worker

    A. gradually move this youth into another group of youths who are *straight*
    B. make the worker realize this is his problem, in his area, and that he must work it out the best way
    C. involve this youth and his group of friends in the programs and activities of the unit
    D. tell the youth he must work this out himself

18. Youth workers must help angry alienated adolescents to learn how to

    A. control their anger by learning when it's worthwhile to get angry
    B. suppress their angry feelings
    C. realize that anger is an unconscious emotion
    D. take part in aggressive demonstrations and takeovers

19. Of the following, an IMPORTANT reason why certain youths are stereotyped by the police and are therefore treated unfairly by them is that

    A. delinquent youths deserve to be treated more severely because they cause trouble for others
    B. these are only allegations and rhetoric made up by revolutionary elements who are hostile to the police
    C. the prevalence of *turnstile justice* results in hasty judgments by the police
    D. police officers in the field have no immediate data concerning the youths' backgrounds and react to their behavior at the moment

20. Group approaches are COMMONLY used for

    A. encounter, discussion, training, and administration
    B. education, counseling, therapy, and recreation
    C. counseling, recreation, catharsis, and crisis intervention
    D. competition, leadership, administration, and training

21. A worker under your supervision is having difficulty reaching some of the youths he is working with on a one-to-one basis. The recording on these youths shows that they have had little opportunity for healthy interpersonal relations.
    You should advise this worker to

    A. involve these youths in group counseling in order to help them overcome their reluctance in sharing experiences with another person
    B. refer these youths for psychiatric services because they are not likely to be reached by a youth worker
    C. assign these youths to Big Brothers or Big Sisters because they need to share a normal family experience
    D. give these youths more time to get to know and trust the worker

22. Planning, organization, methods, direction, coordination, budget and fiscal management, public relations, personnel administration, training, and supervision are the ESSENTIAL elements of

    A. group psychotherapy
    B. ego-oriented casework
    C. consultation
    D. administration

23. If a supervisor is unaware of a new worker's limitations and makes demands which are beyond the worker's capabilities, this will

    A. undermine the worker's confidence in functioning up to the limit of his actual capacities
    B. provide an incentive for the worker to further his training and improve services
    C. demonstrate the need for the agency to provide better orientation and in-service training for staff
    D. encourage the worker to function at a level higher than his present capacities

24. A high government official has announced: *We're looking for possible consolidation of services, for overlapping, for frills, for some built-in bureaucratic procedures that have been kind of historic but that no one has ever taken a long look at to see if time and technology have made them obsolete.*
    For the unit supervisor, the implication of this statement is that it is his responsibility to

    A. ignore this announcement since it pertains to matters beyond his responsibility
    B. report all matters of bureaucratic inefficiency directly to this high government official
    C. inform his workers at a staff meeting that there will be no funds for programs for the next few months
    D. try to involve the staff in a realistic reappraisal of the unit's program and discuss suggestions for cutbacks with the area administrator

25. Assume that you are a new unit supervisor in the Youth Services Agency and your workers bring many grievances to your attention.
    The BEST way for you, the supervisor, to reduce grievances in your unit is to

    A. have the workers submit fully documented written grievances
    B. consider each grievance seriously and eliminate the cause if possible
    C. make workers realize that grievances reflect their immaturity and rejection of authority
    D. refer the workers' grievances to the area Administrator

26. Of the following, BASIC subject areas to be discussed in staff conferences are:

    A. Job responsibilities, agency structure, social work concepts, needs and resources of people
    B. Case-studying, interviewing, individual growth and development, sources of information other than the client
    C. Community resources, work organization, child welfare services, and standards of performance
    D. All of the above

27. The discussion method in teaching provides a way to help staff integrate knowledge and thus make it available for application to day-to-day work.
    To help workers integrate knowledge and develop skill is an IMPORTANT aspect of

    A. professional training
    B. memos, directives, and position papers
    C. staff and individual conferences
    D. job descriptions

28. The subjects of discussion in staff meetings cannot be isolated from what the unit supervisor

    A. thinks is most important
    B. reads in books, journals, etc.
    C. hears at supervisors' meetings
    D. discusses in individual conferences

29. Interplay between persons appears to speed up the learning process; discussion of the material provides an opportunity for a sharing of knowledge and experience and allows for a testing out of new ideas and application of theory.
    These are the objectives for

    A. Sensitivity Training   B. T-Groups
    C. Staff Conferences   D. Administrative Training

30. A leadership which aims to develop the individual staff member's skill and knowledge, and to direct activities of the staff in such a way as to bring about improvements in the agency's services given to the client. This is a description of GOOD

    A. staff development   B. psychological direction
    C. public accountability   D. supervision

31. In addition to familiarity with techniques in administrative planning and professional knowledge, the MOST important element in good supervision in a social agency is skill in

    A. office management   B. human relations
    C. business methods   D. psychological evaluation

32. If an agency does not have clear and specific unit and job functions, the MOST probable result will be

    A. a gross breakdown in services
    B. gaps and overlaps in responsibility and authority
    C. an inability to function according to the city charter
    D. a violation of the union contractual agreement

33. The one of the following which is the MOST important thing for a unit supervisor to keep in mind regarding the organizational structure of his unit is the

    A. preparation of time sheets and monthly reports
    B. two-way communication and maximum delegation
    C. geometric executive relationships
    D. critiques and controls

7 (#2)

34. Budget and fiscal management is one essential practice of administration. 34.____
    A unit supervisor should see budgeting and fiscal management as a

    A. planning instrument
    B. fiscal control
    C. mandate from the civil service commission
    D. prerequisite of a union contractual agreement

35. Public relations with the community is one of the responsibilities of the unit supervisor. 35.____
    Good public relations means

    A. organizing the community to put pressure on officials in behalf of the agency
    B. getting reports from workers about the malcontents in the community and dealing with them in a diplomatic manner
    C. assuring the community that the unit will provide staff to problem areas
    D. getting understanding and cooperation from the community with which the agency is concerned

36. Problems and misunderstandings that arise from the lack of effective intraorganizational 36.____
    communication are apparent in many organizations.
    Of the following, the means to be employed by the unit supervisor to establish effective communication are

    A. supervisory and staff conferences
    B. manuals, bulletins, and periodic reports
    C. bulletin boards, memos, and unit newsletters
    D. all of the above

37. A personnel problem facing supervisors in public service more than in private industry is 37.____

    A. union management and negotiation
    B. budget and fiscal control
    C. systematic selection and tenure
    D. advisory boards and political connections

38. Which of the following three types of records are COMMON to most social agencies? 38.____

    A. Administrative, budgetary, and case
    B. Administrative, statistical, and case
    C. Administrative, budgetary, and statistical
    D. Budgetary, statistical, and case

39. Even after several supervisory conferences on a case, a worker in your unit seems not to 39.____
    be giving effective help. In a burst of anger, the worker tells a coworker that the supervisor expects him to learn in a short time what the supervisor has taken years to learn.
    Of the following, the BEST description of the supervisory relationship here is that the

    A. supervisor is so intent on seeing that the necessary service is given that he is unaware of the worker's inability to perform the service
    B. worker's behavior shows that he is too immature to be working in such a difficult field

C. worker is unaware of casework principles and techniques and their application to such a difficult case
D. supervisor is unable to give the worker effective guidance in the supervisory conference, which indicates that the worker needs academic professional training

40. The one of the following which is NOT an essential ingredient of a good staff development and training program
is that it should

   A. include all members of the agency
   B. meet the specific needs of the staff in relation to their job responsibilities
   C. be a continuing process
   D. give out the necessary rules and regulations of the agency

41. One of the areas in which consultation differs from supervision is that consultation

   A. is not in the direct administrative line of authority
   B. is offered by someone skilled in a specific area
   C. relates to procedure rather than function
   D. requires special training

42. The supervisor should make sure the unit office keeps records about the youths it serves and their families since these records help in diagnosing and understanding the problems.
Of the following, as the PRIMARY source of information for case records, the workers should use

   A. reports from psychiatrists, doctors, etc.
   B. all other agencies involved with the family
   C. teachers, friends, local indigenous leaders
   D. the parents and the youths themselves

43. Statistical records are needed for planning, research, and accountability although many workers feel that statistics are dull and boring. On the unit level, statistics can come alive when they are

   A. recorded in non-technical language
   B. compiled by the unit expert in mathematics
   C. collected selectively and used against a background knowledge of the community
   D. elaborate, detailed, and accurate

44. With the passage of time, case records

   A. become more valuable
   B. decline in usefulness
   C. produce more information
   D. become cumulative records

45. In general, the purpose of a case record is to

   A. improve staff training and development
   B. make statistics pertinent and real
   C. provide data for research
   D. further professional service to a client

46. A unit supervisor finds after an intensive in-service training course in case recording that his workers tend to postpone their recording and summaries.
    The MOST likely explanation for this is that

    A. recording is not valuable enough to waste that amount of time on
    B. sufficient leadership was not given in the development of case records
    C. the workers are too busy in the field to have time to record
    D. the latest trend in social work is towards shorter records

47. A unit supervisor who has fewer youth workers in his unit than he can supervise effectively will be likely to

    A. make his staff overdependent on him
    B. lack the desire to train his workers effectively
    C. confuse his staff because of lack of direction
    D. supervise his staff too closely

48. The one of the following which is MOST likely to be seriously impaired as a result of poor supervision is the

    A. attitude of youth workers
    B. area of inter-departmental relations
    C. maintenance of case records and reports
    D. staff training and development program

49. It is generally good practice for the supervisor to ask for the opinions of his staff members before taking action affecting them.
    The GREATEST disadvantage of following this principle when changing schedules or assignments is that staff may

    A. believe that the supervisor is unable to make his own decisions
    B. take advantage of the opportunity to present grievances during the discussion
    C. be resentful if their suggestions are not accepted
    D. suggest the same action as the supervisor had planned to take

50. The expansion of community relations or human relations units is a development resulting from the ghetto riots of the past few years.
    The MOST important function such a unit can perform is to

    A. preach brotherhood and racial equality
    B. serve as a means for local city agency officials to develop city policy in accordance with local needs
    C. serve as a means of communication between people with grievances and policy makers who can take action
    D. give awards to prominent citizens who have promoted inter-racial understanding

10 (#2)

KEY (CORRECT ANSWERS)

1. D	11. D	21. A	31. B	41. A
2. C	12. A	22. D	32. B	42. D
3. C	13. C	23. A	33. B	43. C
4. C	14. D	24. D	34. A	44. B
5. A	15. D	25. B	35. D	45. D
6. C	16. A	26. D	36. D	46. B
7. D	17. C	27. C	37. C	47. D
8. D	18. A	28. D	38. B	48. A
9. A	19. D	29. C	39. A	49. C
10. C	20. B	30. D	40. A	50. C

EXAMINATION SECTION
TEST 1

DIRECTIONS: Each question or incomplete statement is followed by several suggested answers or completions. Select the one that BEST answers the question or completes the statement. *PRINT THE LETTER OF THE CORRECT ANSWER IN THE SPACE AT THE RIGHT.*

1. The statement that the youth worker may be used by the members of his gang group as a *role model* means MOST NEARLY that the members may

   A. adopt the worker's behavior, attitudes, and beliefs as their own standards
   B. conceal their roles in the gang from the worker in order to gain his acceptance and trust
   C. test the worker by *acting out* on purpose
   D. conceal their roles in the gang from the worker in order to confuse him

   1.____

2. Which of the following statements about the categories of gang members is CORRECT?
   A

   A. peripheral member does not participate in gang conflict with core members
   B. core member is defined as a leader of the gang
   C. peripheral member is an informal gang leader
   D. core member is a full-fledged, accepted member of the gang

   2.____

3. An uncooperative and antagonistic attitude among adult groups toward youth workers seeking to modify criminal patterns of behavior among youth gang groups is MOST likely to be prevalent in a neighborhood where

   A. efforts of youth-serving agencies long established in the community have produced no tangible results
   B. significant segments of the adult population engage in or support various types of criminal activity
   C. powerful middle-class elements of the population refuse to openly admit the existence of anti-social youth groups, for fear of giving the neighborhood a bad reputation
   D. behavior patterns of gang groups are extremely aggressive and destructive of life and property in the neighborhood

   3.____

4. The characteristics of the groups to be served are a major consideration in developing programs for delinquent youth.
   In general, it has been found that the anti-social acts of juvenile delinquents in neighborhoods that are lowest on the socio-economic scale, compared to the anti-social acts of juvenile delinquents in less deprived areas, are

   A. more aggressive   B. less aggressive
   C. more organized   D. easier to control

   4.____

5. The peer group is even more important for the delinquent adolescent who comes from a severely disadvantaged background than for the comparatively normal middle-class adolescent, MAINLY because the peer group provides the delinquent adolescent with

   A. protection from a usually extreme sense of failure resulting from defective family, school, and other relationships

   5.____

B. ways of obtaining needed funds by participating with their peers in such anti-social acts as muggings, robbery, and petty larceny
C. opportunities to participate in recreational activities that are usually available only to middle-class adolescents
D. access to preparation for realistic adult goals in such legitimate occupations as construction worker, dock worker, or other unskilled and semi-skilled jobs

6. A street-based youth services program is more exposed to community view and evaluation than a program based in a community center or other indoor meeting place. Therefore, there is greater risk of community disapproval and loss of support.
Of the following, the BEST way to minimize this risk is for the agency sponsoring a street-based program to

   A. make every effort to withhold information from the community about such incidents as gang fights, homicides, and criminal activities involving youth
   B. interpret the nature of the service to the community clearly and objectively, giving information about both negative and positive results of the program
   C. arrange for neighborhood gang groups to congregate in their clubrooms wherever possible, so that their activities will not be exposed to view
   D. insist that the police enforce strong punitive measures when gang groups commit anti-social acts that may cause community disapproval of a street-based program

7. Which of the following statements about differences in attitudes and reactions toward delinquent behavior is NOT valid?
Behavior

   A. viewed as delinquent in a middle-class neighborhood may not be so regarded in a lower-class neighborhood
   B. considered delinquent in one lower-class neighborhood may be regarded with less concern in another lower-class neighborhood
   C. which a youth worker considers delinquent and attempts to change when he has established a positive relationship with a gang group would be handled differently during his early contacts with the group
   D. which a youth worker considers delinquent and attempts to change during his early contacts with a gang group would be treated more leniently when he has established a positive relationship with the group

8. The area approach to street work is oriented more toward sociological theory than social work. It rests on the assumption that delinquent gangs reflect the normal strivings of groups of youngsters whose opportunities for *acceptable* behavior are limited.
The one of the following which is MOST likely to be the major emphasis of practitioners of the area approach to street work with youth is to

   A. preserve the gang structure and provide intensive supportive counseling services to individual members and their families
   B. undermine the gang structure and provide intensive supportive counseling services to members and their families
   C. preserve the gang structure and provide more opportunities for gang members to channel their behavior into constructive activities
   D. undermine the gang structure and channel the behavior of its members into more constructive activities

9. Research studies have demonstrated that the social health of a community is directly related to the

   A. opportunities available to its residents
   B. effectiveness of the police in the community
   C. number of social, agencies located in the community
   D. influence of community organizations and groups

10. Because of the complexity of interacting forces contributing to the problems of the delinquent, the gang, and the community, the youth worker's efforts frequently meet with failure.
    It is, therefore, IMPORTANT for the supervisor to help his workers to concentrate their efforts with anti-social youth on

    A. attaining appropriate and often reasonably low levels of improvement
    B. helping mainly those group members who are most likely to profit from his attention
    C. protecting the community from the youths' destructive and anti-social acts
    D. referring the most seriously disturbed youths to agencies staffed by psychiatric professionals

11. The PRIMARY concern of the youth worker who uses the group work approach with small gang groups would be the

    A. interrelationship of group members with each other, with their peers and with adults outside the group
    B. background of each group member in terms of his school, unemployment, and family problems
    C. nature and quality of the illegal activities engaged in by the members of the group
    D. attitudes expressed by local police agencies toward this type of approach with anti-social youths

12. For a youth worker to support the efforts of a conventionally oriented subgroup of a gang to break away from the rest of the group would GENERALLY be

    A. *undesirable,* chiefly because the two groups will probably engage in a gang fight if they separate
    B. *desirable,* if the behavior of the largest number of the group members is highly deviant and anti-social
    C. *undesirable,* chiefly because the conventionally oriented subgroup will no longer be able to prevent the highly deviant members from engaging in antisocial activities
    D. *desirable,* if the larger group is cohesive and the behavior of its members is somewhat constructive

13. A *vertical* group of gang members would be structured according to

    A. turf   B. ethnicity   C. age   D. leadership role

14. In terms of helping the group, which of the following types of leadership would generally be considered MOST acceptable for a youth worker to use with a loosely structured, street-oriented group of youths?

    A. Laissez-faire   B. Manipulative   C. Democratic   D. Autocratic

15. According to Richard A. Cloward and Lloyd E. Ohlin, in DELINQUENCY AND OPPORTUNITY, members of a retreatist sub-culture

    A. retreat during rumbles with members of other gangs
    B. are mainly involved in the use of drugs
    C. do not become involved in anti-social activities
    D. seek status through violent activities

16. Medical specialists and other health and community officials have reported that the recent resurgence of youth gangs and youth violence has been accompanied by a

    A. considerable increase in youthful drug addiction and -criminal activity involving drugs
    B. marked decrease in illegitimate pregnancies and requests for abortions from *women's auxiliary* gang members
    C. considerable increase in alcoholism and related illnesses and emergencies involving ghetto youth
    D. marked decrease in overdose cases and other indications of narcotics use

17. An inexperienced youth worker assigned to a large gang group expresses concern to his supervisor about the possibility of gang conflict and doesn't know which of the members should be kept under closest surveillance.
    The supervisor should advise him that is is MOST important to give closest surveillance to the

    A. president
    B. war counselor
    C. core members
    D. peripheral members

18. The author of an early classic text on street gangs in Chicago is

    A. K.H. Rogers
    B. Irving Spergel
    C. F.M. Thrasher
    D. R.K. Merton

19. The members of an anti-social street gang who should be the objects of the MOST serious concern to youth workers are those who characteristically

    A. show an inability to cope effectively with their own impulsive behavior
    B. behave in a friendly, over-solicitous and helpful manner
    C. act bossy and try to convince the worker to accede to their demands
    D. refuse to accept the worker's friendly overtures and offers of assistance

20. The special language used by members of adolescent street gangs typically reflects their roles as alienated youth in a delinquent subculture.
    The one of the following which is NOT a usual characteristic of their vocabulary is

    A. grandiosity
    B. identification with the underdog
    C. possession of values counter to the larger society
    D. denial of reality

21. Assume that it has been decided that the youth services agency will terminate services to the *Lightning Rods,* a gang group which has not been involved in *jitterbugging* for about two years. When the members, who have developed a strong attachment to their worker, learn that soon they will no longer have regular contact with him, they start to fight and become involved in other anti-social incidents again. As a result, the worker tells his supervisor that he believes he should continue his assignment with the group.
The supervisor SHOULD advise the worker to

    A. continue his services and so inform the group
    B. reassure the group that he will be available if needed, even though he will not see them regularly
    C. disregard the recent incidents, since this is the group's way of seeking attention
    D. make a sharp break with the group, and meet with him in order to discuss his apprehension about losing contact with these youths

22. A supervisor has a new worker whose records indicate that he has potential for becoming an excellent staff member. However, when the supervisor observes the worker in the field, he notices that the worker frequently holds back and seems uncertain in handling his group. When the supervisor talks to the worker about this in private, the worker explains that he hesitates because he is *afraid of doing the wrong thing.*
The BEST way for the supervisor to help this worker is to

    A. assign him to another group until he gets more experience
    B. suggest to him that he would feel better if he had professional training
    C. give him reassurance and as much guidance as he needs
    D. go into the field with him to work with his youths so he can learn directly from him

23. Assume that, when a supervisor visits a gang group for the first time, the group reacts to the supervisor in an antagonistic and hostile manner.
It would be ADVISABLE for the supervisor to

    A. stop visiting the group until he learns from their worker that they have a more positive attitude toward him
    B. discuss the situation with the assigned worker and direct him to call the group to a meeting in the unit office
    C. return to visit the group frequently, making friendly approaches until a better relationship is established
    D. take the group on a bus trip to Bear Mountain without their worker in order to foster a better relationship

24. Assume that a consultant, who has been brought in to review programs in a youth services agency unit, tells the supervisor that he has found that several workers have spent program money for their own personal needs. The supervisor should FIRST

    A. recommend that the workers involved be brought up on charges
    B. realize that the consultant's findings may be biased, and take no further action until he hears from central office
    C. accept the consultant's findings, because the consultant has the ultimate responsibility
    D. review his records and discuss the findings with his staff, in order to determine the facts for himself

25. In the course of a field visit to a youth services agency unit, a supervisor learns that a youth worker has been involved sexually with one of the *debs* in his assigned group. Which of the following would be the MOST appropriate action for the supervisor to take?

    A. Suspend the worker immediately
    B. Allow the worker to continue with his assigned group until a hearing is arranged
    C. Confront the worker with his knowledge of the situation and assign him to the office pending further investigation
    D. Confer with the worker and explain that such an involvement will eventually adversely affect his relationship with the group

Questions 26-30.

DIRECTIONS: Questions 26 through 30 are based on the following example of a youth worker's incident report. The report consists of ten numbered sentences, some of which are not consistent with the principles of good report writing.

(1) On the evening of February 24, James and Larry, two members of the *Black Devils,* were entering with a bottle of wine in their hands. (2) It was unusually good wine for these boys to buy. (3) I told them to give me the bottle and they refused, and added that they wouldn't let anyone *put them out.* (4) I told them they were entitled to have a good time, but they could not do it the way they wanted; there were certain rules they had to observe. (5) At this point, James said he had seen me box at camp and suggested that Larry not accept my offer. (6) Then I said firmly that the admission fee did not give them the authority to tell me what to do. (7) I also told them that, if they thought I would fight them over such a matter, they were sadly mistaken. (8) I added, however, that we could go to the gym right now and settle it another way if they wished. (9) Larry immediately said that he was sorry, he had not understood the rules, and he did not want his quarter back. (10) On the other hand, they would not give up their bottle either, so they left the premises.

26. Only material that is relevant to the main thought of a report should be included. Which of the following sentences from the report contains material which is LEAST relevant to this report?
    Sentence

    A. 2   B. 3   C. 8   D. 9

27. A good report should be arranged in logical order. Which of the following sentences from the report does NOT appear in its proper sequence in the report?
    Sentence

    A. 3   B. 5   C. 7   D. 9

28. Reports should include all essential information.
    Of the following, the MOST important fact that is missing from this report is

    A. who was involved in the incident
    B. how the incident was resolved
    C. when the incident took place
    D. where the incident took place

29. The MOST serious of the following faults commonly found in explanatory reports is 29.____

    A. use of slang terms
    B. excessive details
    C. personal bias
    D. redundancy

30. In reviewing a report he has prepared to submit to his superiors, a supervisor finds that his paragraphs are a typewritten page long and decides to make some revisions. Of the following, the MOST important question he should ask about each paragraph is: 30.____

    A. Are the words too lengthy?
    B. Is the idea under discussion too abstract?
    C. Is more than one central thought being expressed?
    D. Are the sentences too long?

KEY (CORRECT ANSWERS)

1.	A	16.	D
2.	D	17.	C
3.	B	18.	C
4.	A	19.	A
5.	A	20.	B
6.	B	21.	B
7.	D	22.	C
8.	C	23.	C
9.	A	24.	D
10.	A	25.	C
11.	A	26.	A
12.	B	27.	B
13.	C	28.	D
14.	C	29.	C
15.	B	30.	C

TEST 2

DIRECTIONS: Each question or incomplete statement is followed by several suggested answers or completions. Select the one that BEST answers the question or completes the statement. *PRINT THE LETTER OF THE CORRECT ANSWER IN THE SPACE AT THE RIGHT.*

1. Of the following, the factor that is MOST critical and MOST likely to influence the success of the youth worker's handling of aggression by gang group members is the

    A. time and place of the aggressive acts by the group members
    B. timing of the worker's action to curb the aggression
    C. number of group members taking part in the aggressive action
    D. availability of resources to distract the gang group members

    1.____

2. When the leadership of a gang is highly negative or delinquent in nature, it is considered ADVISABLE for a worker who has a positive relationship with the group to

    A. assist the group to shift leadership from the delinquency oriented to the more conventionally oriented members
    B. attempt to oust the deviant leaders from the group
    C. give special attention to programs for the conventionally oriented members
    D. report the highly deviant leaders to the authorities in order to destroy their influence with the group

    2.____

3. Of the following, the MOST important function of the central communications system in an area-based youth services unit is to permit the supervisor to

    A. learn where workers are in the field, and advise or direct them as to the most appropriate way of handling an emergency
    B. relay important information about unit activities and programs to higher-level personnel in the central office
    C. inform the community of the activities of the agency and its achievements in curbing delinquent behavior of neighborhood youth
    D. relay information about policies and procedures as well as routine matters to staff based in the field

    3.____

4. Experts have criticized the use of the Glueck Juvenile Delinquency Prediction Table MAINLY because

    A. a child's personality changes during the various stages of growth
    B. statistics are irrelevant when applied to individuals
    C. personnel who use it may not be properly trained
    D. school personnel may not be objective with children identified as potentially delinquent

    4.____

5. Under the present organization of the youth services agency, the basic unit of service is the

    A. central office
    B. technical assistance unit
    C. community planning district
    D. community board

    5.____

6. The function of the *outreach* staff of the youth services agency is to
   A. provide professional casework services and in-service training to unit staff involved in referrals
   B. identify youths in the community with severe behavioral and psychological problems and refer them for professional help
   C. make contacts with community groups and agencies in order to help them administer their own programs
   D. provide youth with opportunities to take part in community planning and make suggestions for their own programs

7. A youth worker who wants to find out whether a youth in his group and his family are registered with other social and health agencies could get this information from the
   A. Community Service Society
   B. Social Service Exchange
   C. Contributors Information Bureau
   D. Council of Voluntary Agencies

8. Assume that the only guidelines used by a youth services agency staff member assigned to evaluate a contract agency were the contract agency's standards for administration, supervision, and programming.
   Of the following, the MOST important guideline omitted by the evaluator relates to the contract agency's
   A. lower-level staff
   B. physical facilities
   C. board of directors
   D. other funding resources

9. The MOST important purpose of social program evaluation as it is carried out in the youth services agency is to
   A. justify current program operations
   B. provide an objective basis for reductions in program funding
   C. introduce youth services agency personnel to profes-sionals in contract agencies
   D. provide an objective basis for decision-making on programs which will provide effective services to youth

10. The one of the following which is NOT usually included as part of the consultation services provided by the youth services agency staff member assigned to evaluate a contract agency is giving
    A. opinion and advice on program content
    B. information on resources in the youth services agency and the community
    C. help with the formulation of program proposals
    D. in-service training to agency staff

Questions 11-15.

DIRECTIONS: Questions 11 through 15 are to be answered SOLELY on the basis of the following passage.

In an attempt to describe what is meant by a delinquent subculture, let us look at some delinquent activities. We usually assume that when people steal things, they steal because they want them to eat or wear or otherwise use them; or because they can sell them; or even - if we are given to a psychoanalytic turn of mind -because on some deep symbolic level the things stolen substitute or stand for something unconsciously desired but forbidden. However, most delinquent gang stealing has no such utilitarian motivation at all. Even where the value of the object stolen is itself a motivating consideration, the stolen sweets are often sweeter than those acquired by more legitimate and prosaic means. In homelier language, stealing *for the hell of it* and apart from considerations of gain and profit is a valued activity to which attaches glory, prowess, and profound satisfaction.

Similarly, many other delinquent activities are motivated mainly by an enjoyment in the distress of others and by a hostility toward non-gang peers as well as adults. Apart from the more dramatic manifestations in the form of gang wars, there is keen delight in terrorizing *good* children and in driving them from playgrounds and gyms for which the gang itself may have little use. The same spirit is evident in playing hooky and in misbehavior in school. The teacher and her rules are not merely to be evaded. They are to be flouted.

All this suggests that the delinquent subculture is not only a set of rules, a design for living which is different from or indifferent to or even in conflict with the norms of the *respectable* adult society. It actually takes its norms from the larger culture but turns them upside down. The delinquent's conduct is right, by the standards of his subculture, precisely because it is wrong by the standards of the larger culture.

11. Of the following, the MOST suitable title for the above passage is

    A. DIFFERENT KINDS OF DELINQUENT SUBCULTURES
    B. DELINQUENT HOSTILITY TOWARD NON-GANG PEERS
    C. METHODS OF DELINQUENT STEALING
    D. DELINQUENT STANDARDS AS REVEALED BY THEIR ACTIVITIES

12. It nay be inferred from the passage that MOST delinquent stealing is motivated by a

    A. need for food and clothing
    B. need for money to buy drugs
    C. desire for peer-approval
    D. symbolic identification of the thing stolen with hidden desires

13. The passage IMPLIES that an important reason why delinquents play hooky and misbehave in school is that the teachers

    A. represent *respectable* society
    B. are boring
    C. have not taught them the values of the adult society
    D. are too demanding

14. In the passage, the author's attitude toward delinquents is

    A. critical   B. objective
    C. overly sympathetic   D. confused

15. According to the passage, which of the following statements is CORRECT? 15._____

    A. Delinquents derive no satisfaction from stealing.
    B. Delinquents are not hostile toward someone without a reason.
    C. The common motive of many delinquent activities is a desire to frustrate others.
    D. The delinquent subculture shares its standards with the *respectable* adult culture.

Questions 16-18.

DIRECTIONS: Questions 16 through 18 are to be answered SOLELY on the basis of the following paragraph.

A fundamental part of the youth worker's role is changing the interaction patterns which already exist between the delinquent group and the representatives of key institutions in the community, e.g., the policeman, teacher, social worker, employer, parent, and storekeeper. This relationship, particularly its definitional character, is a *two-way* proposition. The offending youth or group will usually respond by fulfilling this prophecy. In the same way, the delinquent expects punishment or antagonistic treatment from officials and other representatives of middle class society; in turn, the adult concerned may act to fulfill the prophecy of the delinquent. Stereotyped patterns of expectation, both of the delinquents and those in contact with them, must be changed. The worker can be instrumental in changing these patterns.

16. Of the following, the MOST suitable title for the paragraph is 16._____

    A. WAYS TO PREDICT JUVENILE DELINQUENCY
    B. THE YOUTH WORKER'S ROLE IN CREATING STEREOTYPES
    C. THE YOUTH WORKER'S ROLE IN CHANGING STEREOTYPED PATTERNS OF EXPECTATION
    D. THE DESIRABILITY OF INTERACTION PATTERNS

17. According to the paragraph, a youth who misbehaves and is told by an agency worker that *his group is a menace to the community* would PROBABLY eventually respond by 17._____

    A. withdrawing into himself
    B. continuing to misbehave
    C. making a greater attempt to please
    D. acting indifferent

18. In this paragraph, the author's opinion about stereotypes is that they are 18._____

    A. *useful,* primarily because they are usually accurate
    B. *useful,* primarily because they make a quick response easier
    C. *harmful,* primarily because the adult community will be less aware of delinquents as a group
    D. *harmful,* primarily because they influence behavior

Questions 19-20.

DIRECTIONS: Questions 19 and 20 are to be answered SOLELY on the basis of the following paragraph.

A drug-user does not completely retreat from society. While a new user, he must begin participation in some group of old users in order to secure access to a steady supply of drugs. In the process, his readiness to engage in drug use, which stems from his personality and the social structure, is reinforced by new patterns of associations and values. The more the individual is caught in this web of associations, the more likely it is that he will persist in drug use, for he has become incorporated into a subculture that exerts control over his behavior. However, it is also true that the resulting tics among addicts are not as strong as those among participants in criminal and conflict subcultures. Addiction is in many ways an individualistic adaptation, for the *kick* is essentially a private experience. The compelling need for the drug is also a divisive force, for it leads to intense competition among addicts for money. Forces of this kind thus limit the relative cohesion which can develop among users.

19. According to the paragraph, the MAIN reason why new drug users associate with old users is a

    A. fear of the police
    B. common hatred of society
    C. need to get drugs
    D. dislike of being alone

20. According to the paragraph, which of the following statements is INCORRECT?

    A. Drug users encourage each other to continue taking drugs.
    B. Gangs that use drugs are more cohesive than other delinquent gangs.
    C. A youth's desire to use drugs stems from his personality as well as the social structure.
    D. Addicts get no more of a *kick* from using drugs in a group than alone.

21. The MOST appropriate of the following methods for a supervisor to use FIRST in order to become knowledgeable about a gang group assigned to one of his workers is to

    A. work with the group on the worker's scheduled days off
    B. read the worker's recordings and discuss the group with the worker in supervisory conferences
    C. observe the worker in the field as he interacts with group members
    D. accompany the group on trips and other programmed activities

22. Assume that a supervisor has been assigned to take workers into a community which is in an uproar as a result of a recent outbreak of gang conflict during which a youth was killed. There were no youth services agency units or street workers in this community previously. The supervisor SHOULD approach this situation by

    A. calling a meeting with representatives of all the gang groups in order to assess the situation and discuss possible ways of curbing the conflicts
    B. contacting the police precinct for information about the hangouts of the gangs
    C. assigning workers to contact gang groups and urge them to move their activities out of the neighborhood
    D. meeting with the neighborhood leaders, staff of community organizations and other social agencies to discuss the magnitude of the problem and to mobilize resources

23. As a result of longstanding resentment between two gangs covered by a supervisor's unit, a popular youth who belonged to a third gang group was shot to death by accident. How should the supervisor handle this crisis?

A. Immediately call a meeting of all the gang groups in the area to assess their feelings about the youth's death
B. Mobilize unit workers to cover as many groups as possible, in order to be able to monitor their movements and plans
C. Submit requests for buses to remove the two hostile groups from the area
D. Request assistance from members of neighborhood auxiliary police in the area

24. In the course of a field visit, a supervisor learns for the first time that a worker has been discussing a weekend trip to Philadelphia with his assigned group when several youths in the group come up to him and ask for his deci-sion on the trip.
The BEST course of action for the supervisor to take Would be to tell the youth that   24._____

    A. he approves of the trip, so that the youths will not be frustrated
    B. he disapproves of the trip, so that the worker will learn to request approval before getting the youths excited about a trip
    C. the worker did not discuss the trip with him, but that the worker will have to make the decision anyway
    D. he is still considering the trip, and will evaluate it later on its own merits

25. It is frequently difficult for a supervisor to convince youth workers assigned to street gangs of the importance of recording.
While training his workers in proper recording methods, the supervisor should emphasize that, of the following, the MOST important purpose of recording is to   25._____

    A. evaluate progress made by groups and individual members
    B. determine the effectiveness of the agency as a whole
    C. identify flaws in on-going programs
    D. plan future programs

Questions 26-30.

DIRECTIONS: In Questions 26 through 30, choose the lettered word or expression which is closest to the meaning of the first word or expression, *as used most frequently by street-oriented youths and members of youth gangs.* Do not try to give the usually accepted or dictionary definition of the word or expression.

26. wig out   26._____

    A. shoplift clothes   B. engage in homosexuality
    C. feel shocked   D. refuse to use drugs

27. dipple   27._____

    A. cocaine user   B. former hippie
    C. unit of drugs   D. nervous junkie

28. flaky   28._____

    A. a little abnormal mentally
    B. nervy
    C. enjoyable
    D. beaten to a pulp

29. wag tail
    A. succeed   B. conform   C. fool   D. inform

30. dolphins
    A. amphetamines   B. suspicious pushers
    C. methadone pills   D. pimps

KEY (CORRECT ANSWERS)

1. B
2. A
3. A
4. D
5. C

6. B
7. B
8. A
9. D
10. D

11. D
12. C
13. A
14. B
15. C

16. C
17. B
18. D
19. C
20. B

21. B
22. D
23. B
24. D
25. A

26. C
27. B
28. A
29. B
30. C

EXAMINATION SECTION
TEST 1

DIRECTIONS: Each question or incomplete statement is followed by several suggested answers or completions. Select the one that BEST answers the question or completes the statement. *PRINT THE LETTER OF THE CORRECT ANSWER IN THE SPACE AT THE RIGHT.*

1. A youth worker asks his supervisor what to do about his gang group whose members have informed him that they are planning to *go down* on another group for *jumping* one of their members on his way home from school.
It would be best for the supervisor to recommend that the worker should FIRST

    A. individually question the members of his group about the incident
    B. engage the group members in activities outside of the neighborhood
    C. arrange a mediation meeting involving both groups
    D. report the information to police to avoid further trouble

2. A youth worker tells his supervisor that the owner of a local bowling alley has asked him to bring his gang group over for recreation. A financial arrangement beneficial to the worker was suggested as part of the plan.
The supervisor should advise the worker to

    A. refuse the offer because he should avoid entanglements that might compromise the agency or his professional conduct
    B. refuse the offer because he should avoid contact with the business community
    C. accept the offer but refuse payment because he should utilize all resources offered to gang members
    D. accept the offer but refuse payment because he can use the situation to establish a relationship with a member of the business community

3. Assume that a youth worker who previously had important responsibilities complains to his supervisor about having to share periodic office coverage. This employee has been back for a few months after a serious illness and is not yet able to resume all of his previous responsibilities, but is well enough to function as a worker.
The BEST way for the supervisor to handle this complaint is to

    A. refer the problem to his area administrator because of the special nature of the case
    B. excuse the employee from office coverage
    C. suggest to the employee that he may be well enough to take on his previous responsibilities again
    D. tell the employee that office coverage must be shared by all workers in the unit

4. During a unit staff meeting, several youth workers raise objections to a certain youth services agency policy and make suggestions for revision of the policy that seem to the supervisor to have considerable merit.
The MOST appropriate action for the supervisor to take would be to

A. allow the workers to interpret the policy according to their suggestions, which relate to the needs of this neighborhood
B. inform the workers that policy changes must be initiated and implemented by higher administrative personnel of the agency
C. help the workers prepare a proposal outlining their suggestions to be submitted by the unit to higher administrative personnel
D. report to his administrator that his workers object to the policy and that considerable revision is required

5. Which of the following methods available to the supervisor of youth workers is usually MOST effective in facilitating communication with his subordinates?

   A. Weekly staff meetings B. Memoranda
   C. Unscheduled conferences D. Work shops

6. Several youths who belong to a gang group come to the supervisor with a problem that should have been handled by their assigned youth worker. As they talk to the supervisor, the youths also make strong complaints about their worker.
Of the following, it would be advisable for the supervisor to

   A. ignore the complaints at this time because it is risky to accept reports from gang members without further investigation
   B. report the incident to the area administrator and ask him to deal administratively with this worker
   C. review the worker's records and discuss the problem with him and the youths before taking further action
   D. have the worker transferred to another unit because he seems to be in danger of attack by these youths

7. Of the following, the factor that the supervisor should consider MOST important in evaluating a youth worker's performance is

   A. how frequently he asks for guidance
   B. his willingness to be helpful and cooperative
   C. his consistency in keeping his recording up to date
   D. his interest in his group members and his effectiveness in dealing with them

8. Assume that a citizens' group addresses a letter of commendation to a supervisor praising the youth workers on his staff for their extraordinary service in helping to deal with several emergencies involving youth in the area.
Of the following, it would be advisable for the supervisor to FIRST

   A. send the letter to the director of field operations
   B. call in the staff member who was most helpful and commend him in private
   C. write a letter of thanks to the citizens' group in the name of his staff
   D. share this commendation with his staff and his area administrator

9. A worker reports to his supervisor that one of his group members has begun to experiment with marijuana. The worker feels uneasy about handling the situation and asks for guidance.
   The supervisor should advise the worker to

   A. ignore the situation since most youths experiment with marijuana
   B. refer the youth to a drug prevention program
   C. confront the youth and discuss the situation with him
   D. discuss the situation with the youth's parents

10. In a supervisory conference, a worker asks for guidance about how to handle the problem of a 22-year-old dropout who wants to return to school in the daytime to obtain a high school diploma so that he can apply to a community college. The worker has contacted the youth's former school, but the principal refuses to take the youth back because of his age.
    Of the following, the supervisor's BEST approach would be to advise the worker to

    A. contact the district school superintendent's office and request an exception in the case of this youth
    B. tell the youth's parents to submit an appeal to the Board of Education
    C. refer the youth to a vocational training program instead
    D. urge the youth to attend evening high school and work during the day

11. A youth worker tells his superior he has definite evidence that one of his group members is *dealing*, but hesitates to identify the youth because he does not want to violate the principle of confidentiality.
    The supervisor should

    A. give the worker a direct order to identify the youth and take disciplinary action if the worker refuses
    B. reassign this worker to another group since he seems to be over-identifying with this youth
    C. discuss with the worker the reasons for reporting illegal acts and clarify agency policy and the need to enforce it
    D. visit and observe the group himself in order to identify the youth who is *dealing*

12. During his review of workers' recordings, a supervisor finds that one of his workers refers most youths who ask him about employment to a job placement agency after interviewing them only once.
    Of the following, the BEST advice the supervisor can give this worker is:

    A. Workers should try to find suitable openings in the neighborhood before referring youths to a job placement agency
    B. As a rule, a worker should interview youths seeking employment more than once in order to determine their needs and prepare them before referring them to an outside agency
    C. The youths are probably asking the worker to help them find employment in order to get attention and emotional support and are not really ready to get jobs
    D. Workers should make every effort to convince youths to go back to school and refer them for jobs only as a last resort

13. In a discussion with her supervisor about one of her group members, a female youth worker reports that she is planning to encourage 18-year-old Maria, who was born in Puerto Rico and is employed, to leave home because her father is very domineering. It would be appropriate for the supervisor to

    A. support the worker because an 18-year-old girl who has a job needs to be more independent
    B. advise the worker not to encourage Maria to leave home at this time and refer Maria's father to a casework agency
    C. advise the worker not to encourage Maria to leave home and try to help Maria's mother to assert a more active role
    D. determine whether the worker realizes that Maria's father may be assuming the patriarchal role which would be traditional for him

14. A youth worker tells his supervisor that he feels that he does not have enough leeway in serving his group and must rigidly follow too many regulations and procedures.
    Of the following, the BEST way for the supervisor to help this worker is to

    A. tell him that as long as he uses good judgment he need not worry about regulations and procedures
    B. compliment the worker whenever he interprets regulations and procedures less rigidly
    C. ask him for program suggestions and assure him that his ideas will be considered
    D. give him additional authority and responsibility

15. A supervisor learns that a youth worker with considerable experience has recently been acting hostile to his group and has not been providing services requested by the members.
    The supervisor's FIRST action should be to discuss this behavior with the worker and

    A. suggest that he consult with a therapist about his unconscious motives
    B. try to help him understand why he is acting hostile
    C. suggest to him that he may not like the group
    D. point out that the group may not react to the worker's hostility

16. A youth worker asks his supervisor for guidance about a 15-year-old youth who had been one of the most constructive members of his group, but has recently been getting into trouble. The youth's father died ten years ago, and his mother has just remarried.
    The supervisor should help the worker to realize that the youth

    A. is probably going through a crisis and should be given special attention
    B. probably dislikes his stepfather and is misbehaving in the hope of being placed away from home
    C. will stop misbehaving if his present conduct is not taken too seriously
    D. should be warned that further misbehavior must be reported to his stepfather

17. During a weekly conference with his supervisor, a worker reports that a youth in his group has told him that his father is *messing around* with his 13-year-old sister. When the sister confided in the youth, she said that the father threatened to kill her if she told anyone that he was having sex with her, and the youth is frightened.
The supervisor should FIRST

   A. call the father into his office on the pretext of discussing the youth's problems in order to assess the situation
   B. have the worker report the situation to the local juvenile aid police officer
   C. have the worker report the situation immediately to the local child protective services unit of the Bureau of Child Welfare
   D. call the sister into the office in order to obtain the facts for himself

18. A youth worker who has a friend in central office is continually spreading rumors that he claims to have heard from his *connections downtown*. These rumors often sound true and are upsetting to staff.
The MOST advisable action for the supervisor of this unit to take at this point would be to

   A. tell his staff to disregard the stories spread by this worker
   B. report the worker to the director of field operations and request that he be reprimanded for his behavior
   C. arrange the worker's assignments so that he will have nothing more to do with central office
   D. tell the worker privately that his rumors are creating a morale problem and he must stop spreading them at once

19. A supervisor of a youth services unit has interviewed the father of an 18-year-old youth who says that the boy has been stealing, moody, and *hangs around with a bunch of no-good junkies*. The supervisor has reason to believe that the boy is experimenting with hard drugs, but the father does not seem to be able to cope with this because of his fears and his pride in the family.
When the supervisor assigns a worker to this case, it would be appropriate for him to tell the worker to start out by

   A. telling the father that the boy is on hard drugs and should be in treatment
   B. suggesting to the father to have the boy put under observation by the youth division of the police department
   C. talking with the father about widespread drug use and narcotic addiction among middle-class youth in order to relieve him of his guilt
   D. assuring the father that confidentiality will be upheld and that he should feel free to discuss his fears

20. A supervisor finds it necessary to intervene in a heated argument between two of his workers. One worker, who comes from a middle class background, insists that drug abuse is due mainly to psychological problems, while the other worker, who was brought up in the ghetto, insists that drug abuse is due to the pressures of *the street*.
The BEST way for the supervisor to handle this dispute would be to

    A. assign the middle-class worker to the office since he is probably having difficulty working in the street
    B. tell the workers to *cool it* and separate them in their assignments in the field
    C. help the workers to see that both are partly right and could probably learn from each other if they could manage to have a calm discussion
    D. give both workers reliable literature on drug abuse so that they will get the facts in proper perspective

20.____

Questions 21-30.

DIRECTIONS: In Questions 21 through 30, choose the lettered word or expression which is CLOSEST to the meaning of the first word or expression, *as used most frequently by street-oriented youths and members of youth gangs*. Do not try to give the usually accepted or dictionary definition of the word or expression.

21. *dyke*

    A. *crack* package   B. packet of narcotics
    C. opium addict   D. female homosexual

21.____

22. *burned out*

    A. kicked the habit   B. took an overdose
    C. pulled a robbery   D. challenged a rival gang

22.____

23. *drop acid*

    A. buy LSD   B. take LSD
    C. stay off LSD   D. sell LSD

23.____

24. *juicehead*

    A. homosexual   B. natural food faddist
    C. *ice* user   D. alcoholic

24.____

25. *threads*

    A. popped veins   B. police connections
    C. complications   D. clothes

25.____

26. *out of sight*

    A. conventional   B. superb
    C. informed   D. forbidden

26.____

27. *hairy*

    A. difficult   B. smart
    C. torn into shreds   D. mentally disturbed

27.____

28. *blowing snow*

    A. cheating
    C. sniffing cocaine
    B. giving up
    D. keeping secret

28._____

29. *feed your head*

    A. steal food
    C. act crazy
    B. fall asleep
    D. take drugs

29._____

30. *racked up*

    A. taken an overdose
    C. upset
    B. drunk
    D. hiding from the police

30._____

KEY (CORRECT ANSWERS)

1. A	11. C	21. D
2. A	12. B	22. A
3. D	13. D	23. B
4. C	14. C	24. D
5. A	15. B	25. D
6. C	16. A	26. B
7. D	17. C	27. A
8. D	18. D	28. C
9. C	19. D	29. D
10. D	20. C	30. C

TEST 2

DIRECTIONS: Each question or incomplete statement is followed by several suggested answers or completions. Select the one that BEST answers the question or completes the statement. *PRINT THE LETTER OF THE CORRECT ANSWER IN THE SPACE AT THE RIGHT.*

1. A youth comes running into the unit office and reports that a Black youth has been killed in a fight between Black and Asian gang members and that Black adults in the community are in an uproar and are threatening violence against Asians.
   Of the following, the supervisor should FIRST

   A. call Black and Asian adult community leaders into his office in order to enlist their help in preventing further violence
   B. assign as many Black and Asian workers as possible to the respective gang groups in an attempt to *cool it*
   C. get immediate field reports from workers in the affected areas in order to get an accurate picture of the situation
   D. call Black and Asian gang leaders into his office for a mediation meeting

2. The *Social Seven*, a gang group, have not had a gang fight for the past 16 months, and most of the members have not been involved in any other anti-social incidents recently. The assigned worker suggests termination of services to this group and asks his supervisor to be reassigned to the *Spanish Lads*, a real *down* group.
   The appropriate action for the supervisor to take at this point would be to

   A. reassign the worker since the *Social Seven* are not likely to get into trouble at this stage
   B. keep the worker with the *Social Seven* since a gang group's behavior is unpredictable
   C. set up meetings with the worker to discuss the pros and cons of termination of services to the *Social Seven*
   D. advise the worker to continue working with the *Social Seven* but to make less contact with them and drift away gradually

3. A 15-year-old youth who attends high school comes into the office at a time when he should be on his way to school and asks for help in finding a part-time job after school.
   The BEST way for the worker to handle this situation is to

   A. interview the youth about a job so that he does not waste the day
   B. refuse to interview the youth at the time and advise him to go to school and return at the end of the day
   C. interview the youth and determine his reasons for wanting a job
   D. phone the youth's parents and advise them that the youth is out of school that day

4. A worker has had considerable discussion with a youth about his problems and decides that he should be referred to another agency for special treatment.
   Which of the following would be the MOST appropriate way for the worker to handle the referral?

   A. Send the youth to the agency with a brief note since the youth can best explain his problems.
   B. Phone the intake worker of the agency to discuss the youth's case and have the agency make the initial contact with the youth.
   C. Talk to the youth about the referral process before and after making contact and discussing the youth's case with a representative of the agency.
   D. Offer the youth a choice of several suitable agencies and have him make the initial contact.

5. After preparing a youth for referral to a treatment center, a youth worker should usually maintain close contact with both the youth and his therapist.
   This continued contact is important MAINLY because the

   A. worker will be able to take the supportive role needed to keep the youth in treatment
   B. youth will be able to get a more realistic picture of the treatment process
   C. worker will have a chance to get first-hand knowledge about the treatment process
   D. therapist will have a chance to meet the worker

6. In order to make suitable referrals and use community agencies to the greatest extent possible, it is MOST important for the youth worker to know

   A. what services the agencies have to offer
   B. the locations of the central offices of the agencies
   C. how the agencies are funded
   D. prominent staff members of the agencies

7. A supervisor who has been working with his staff to implement a job program for youths in his area drafts a program proposal to submit to the director of field operations. The items covered in the proposal are resources, population to be served, priorities, role of the agency, participation of the community in the program, staff needs, and budget needs.
   Of the following, a KEY factor which has been OMITTED is

   A. names of interested community leaders
   B. documentation of need for the program
   C. approval of the unit staff
   D. approval of the community

8. A worker comes to his supervisor for help in handling the problem of a 14-year-old youth who is talking about *splitting* from home. The worker has developed a close relationship with this youth and his family and does not consider the situation to be serious enough to justify the youth's desire to leave home.
It would be advisable for the supervisor to

   A. help the worker to see that he is over-identifying with the youth and his family and should become less involved
   B. have the worker contact the youth division in the local precinct because experience indicates that this youth will probably run away from home
   C. discuss with the worker some specific ways to help this youth by *talking it out* with him and his parents
   D. help the worker to see that this is a big *put on* by the youth to get attention

9. An inexperienced female youth worker in a supervisor's unit has been working with a group of 13- to 15-year-old girls. The worker's records indicate that whenever the girls start talking about sex, having babies, and abortions, the worker becomes very formal and does her best to get them to change the subject.
The supervisor should

   A. encourage the worker to continue to act as an authority figure with the girls and to avoid talking about sex with them
   B. realize that the worker has a hang-up about sex and is unlikely to be able to handle girls with precocious sexual knowledge and behavior
   C. tell the worker that she is being too hard on these girls and will have a better relationship with them if she can talk about sex on their level
   D. realize that the girls may be *testing* the worker and that she may not be confident enough to handle this yet and needs the supervisor's help and support

10. A youth worker in a supervisor's unit is unusually outspoken and assertive and often gets into heated discussions with colleagues in the unit and youth workers from other agencies over services the worker feels are needed by his group.
The BEST way for the supervisor to attempt to resolve this problem is to

    A. help the other workers in the unit to stay *cool* when this worker gets excited about his group's unmet needs
    B. have the worker transferred to another unit
    C. help the worker to become more diplomatic with colleagues and representatives of outside agencies
    D. encourage the worker to keep being assertive because it is the only way to get results

11. A recently arrived Hispanic youth who speaks no English comes to a youth services agency office asking for help in finding employment.
The supervisor's FIRST step should be to

    A. refer the youth to an employment agency where Spanish is spoken
    B. refer the youth to a program for learning English as a second language
    C. assign a Spanish-speaking worker to interview the youth and evaluate his needs
    D. assign the youth to a worker and suggest that a job be developed for the youth where English will not be needed

12. As a result of several meetings held with neighborhood residents by a youth worker, the community is becoming more interested in problems of local youths. After several months, the community group makes a request through the worker for help from the youth services agency in establishing a small, locally-run youth center.
It would be BEST for the youth worker's supervisor to

    A. suggest to the worker that the program plan may be premature
    B. tell the worker to advise the community group to raise funds for the center in the neighborhood
    C. have the worker help the group to prepare their program request for submission to higher levels in the agency
    D. submit the community's plan to the program planning committee

13. Of the following, the CHIEF cause of death among people between 15-25 years of age is

    A. lead poisoning
    B. drug abuse
    C. suicide
    D. malnutrition

14. Some psychiatrists and psychologists have a low opinion of the street club worker's function and his value in changing the behavior of anti-social youths.
Of the following, the MOST serious consequence of such an attitude is that it may

    A. cause street club workers to resent other professionals
    B. discourage street club workers from referring youths to psychologists and psychiatrists
    C. result in transference of this negative attitude about street club workers to their group members
    D. make it difficult for street club workers to obtain professional training

15. Assume that the unit supervisor observes that a youth who is waiting in the office for his first interview with a worker is nervous, sweating, yawning, and constantly blowing his nose.
It would be important for the supervisor to

    A. discuss his observations and possible reasons for the youth's behavior with the worker who interviews him
    B. call the youth into his office for a brief talk in order to observe him more closely
    C. greet the youth casually and try to put him at ease before the interview
    D. discuss the youth's behavior with him at length before he is interviewed by the worker

16. Assume that a group of mothers comes to the local youth services agency office with the complaint that their pre-adolescent children are in danger of getting into trouble because there are very few recreational facilities available for them in the neighborhood. They ask the supervisor for his help in developing more recreational resources.
Of the following, the MOST appropriate action for the supervisor to take FIRST would be to

    A. refer the matter to the department of recreation
    B. discuss the request with administrative officials of the youth services agency
    C. discuss the situation with workers assigned in the neighborhood since they should have pertinent information about recreational facilities
    D. invite mothers to a meeting with other interested community people in an effort to properly identify the problem

17. The president of the neighborhood block association invites the supervisor of the local youth services agency unit for the first time to a meeting called to discuss community problems caused by the anti-social behavior of gang youth in the area.
The supervisor should welcome the opportunity to attend this meeting MAINLY because it would enable him to

    A. gain some insight into the feelings of neighborhood adults about gang youths and explain to them how agency workers relate to anti-social youths
    B. gain additional insight into the gang members' feelings and concerns about neighborhood adults
    C. assure members of the block association that the youth services agency is making substantial progress in curbing anti-social behavior of local youth
    D. gather specific complaints from neighborhood adults about the behavior of individual youths so that he can assign workers to give additional attention to curbing their anti-social acts

18. Assume that a youth worker newly assigned to a gang group becomes friendly with Dano a member of the group, and wants Dano to help him make his first contacts with the other members.
Before proceeding further, it is important for the worker to

    A. inform Dano that he has been assigned to the area by the youth services agency to work with the group
    B. question Dano about the group without identifying himself as a representative of the youth services agency
    C. talk about sports and other matters that would interest Dano and give no indication that he is a youth worker assigned to the group
    D. ask Dano to arrange for the worker to meet with the group as a whole

19. Assume that a youth worker recently assigned to a gang group has been able to make friends with a few of the members individually. However, the more powerful members of the group seem to resent his presence in the area.
At this point, the worker should

    A. continue to relate to the individual members of the group
    B. try to convince the leader of the group that he can do a lot for them
    C. leave the area because he may be in danger of physical attack by the hostile members
    D. invite the entire group to go out with him for refreshments

20. A youth worker reports to his assigned area and is told by one of his gang group members that the group is angry with him and wants him to leave the neighborhood.
The worker can BEST approach this situation by

    A. locating the other members and trying to find out what their attitude is toward him
    B. leaving the neighborhood for the day in the hope that the situation will resolve itself
    C. asking his supervisor for temporary reassignment to another group until the hostile members *cool off*
    D. arranging an informal gathering with refreshments and inviting the hostile members

21. Several workers present their supervisor with excellent proposals for programs with their assigned groups. However, the supervisor finds that staff and budget resources are far from adequate to implement these programs as planned by the workers.
    Of the following, it would usually be advisable for the supervisor to

    A. request additional funds to carry out the programs
    B. ask the workers to review the programs and resubmit them after making revisions wherever possible to reduce staff and funding requirements
    C. approve the programs on a priority basis, implementing first those planned for the groups with the most serious problems
    D. ask his administrator for guidance on how to allocate staff and funds

21._____

22. A supervisor has been directed by his area administrator to assign one of his workers to a special task to be completed within a month and gives the assignment to a worker whom he considers most capable of doing the job. The worker seems hesitant but accepts the assignment without comment, even though he is told that he will be relieved of some of his regular work. However, when the supervisor checks on the worker's progress a week later, he finds that he has not started to work on the assignment.
    The BEST action for the supervisor to take is to

    A. give part of the assignment to another worker since it must be completed to meet the deadline
    B. report the worker to the area administrator for insubordination
    C. remind the worker about the assignment and assure him of your confidence that he will complete it on time
    D. reassign the entire task to another worker

22._____

23. Assume that the supervisor of a youth services agency unit makes demands upon a new worker which are beyond the worker's present capabilities.
    Of the following, the MOST probable result of the supervisor's actions would be to

    A. give the worker an incentive to learn at a faster pace
    B. undermine the worker's confidence and inhibit him from fulfilling his present capabilities
    C. demonstrate the need for formal in-service training before a new worker is assigned to a unit
    D. encourage the worker to seek professional training in order to improve his performance

23._____

24. A worker reports to his supervisor that one of the subgroups in a youth council is led by a youth who has many constructive ideas but whose contribution is limited because of his rivalry with the elected president of the council.
    Of the following, the supervisor should advise the worker to

    A. allow the youths to settle this problem without outside assistance
    B. tell the leader of the sub-group to withhold his ideas until he becomes an elected officer
    C. attempt to curb the rivalry so that the leader of the sub-group can get his ideas across
    D. appoint the leader of the sub-group to the executive board of the council

24._____

25. A worker tells his supervisor that he is troubled because the youths in his group are continually asking him personal questions, and he does not know how to answer them.
Of the following, it would be BEST for the supervisor to advise the worker to

   A. try to find out why the youths are asking these questions
   B. point out to the youths that it would not be professional to answer personal questions
   C. try to give a brief, truthful answer and immediately redirect the youths to their own problems
   D. tell the youths everything they want to know in order to foster a friendly relationship

26. The supervisor should advise new staff members that, in working with adolescent groups, it is important for the worker to give guidance

   A. at every opportunity
   B. only when the members ask for it
   C. without becoming the group leader himself
   D. to a greater extent to the less aggressive members

27. A youth worker reports to his supervisor that the behavior of the youths in his group is fairly orderly while he is with them, but that roughhousing breaks out as soon as he leaves them.
Of the following, the MOST reasonable explanation for this change in their behavior is that

   A. the worker is not exercising enough control
   B. this is the typical behavior pattern of anti-social youth
   C. the worker is probably too strict and *tight* with them
   D. the youths dislike the worker and resent his presence

28. Most adolescents hesitate to risk disapproval by showing their fears and anxieties. However, repressing these fears and anxieties may lead to more serious psychological problems.
The one of the following which would be the MOST appropriate method for a youth worker to use in order to help his group overcome their fears and anxieties would be to schedule

   A. regular sessions during which the members are encouraged to discuss their fears and anxieties
   B. activities that are not likely to produce fears and anxieties
   C. programs that give special emphasis to wrestling, boxing, and competitive sports
   D. talks by professionals on typical adolescent fears and anxieties

29. In attempting to achieve constructive goals by means of programs, it is particularly important for the youth worker to be aware that delinquent youths

   A. are usually more interested in activities that take them away from their immediate neighborhood
   B. tend to *act out* feelings and express themselves by means of activity rather than verbal exchange
   C. tend to participate more actively if the youth worker takes a passive role while the program is in progress
   D. are best suited to activities that require considerable sharing and integration of effort

30. According to observers of present-day gang groups, the gang leaders often choose a member who is a minor to commit a crime for the group as a whole.
    The MOST plausible reason why the gang would make such a choice is that a minor is

    A. usually stereotyped by the police
    B. less likely to receive a long prison sentence
    C. more likely to be released on his own recognizance
    D. easier to hide from the police

30.____

KEY (CORRECT ANSWERS)

1. C	11. C	21. B
2. C	12. C	22. C
3. B	13. B	23. B
4. C	14. B	24. C
5. A	15. A	25. C
6. A	16. D	26. C
7. B	17. A	27. C
8. C	18. A	28. A
9. D	19. A	29. B
10. C	20. A	30. B

EXAMINATION SECTION
TEST 1

DIRECTIONS: Each question or incomplete statement is followed by several suggested answers or completions. Select the one that BEST answers the question or completes the Statement. *PRINT THE LETTER OF THE CORRECT ANSWER IN THE SPACE AT THE RIGHT.*

1. Perhaps the GREATEST single element in the beginning stages of work with a group is the   1._____

    A. attainment of respect and almost "blind faith" on the part of the group
    B. worker's ability to accept the group "as it is"
    C. possession of a broad sense of humor
    D. ability to bring together members with similar problems and personality traits
    E. ability to raise enough money to support the group properly

2. The ONLY way in which a group worker can determine the stage of development of the group is to   2._____

    A. study the behavior of each individual member of the group
    B. study the behavior responses of the group individually and collectively
    C. discontinue the "pre-group" stages temporarily and study the reaction
    D. ask each member individually what his feelings are on the subject
    E. consult the records of the group

3. All groups at one time or another feel hostile toward their worker or agency, and such behavior is   3._____

    A. dangerous and must be suppressed at once
    B. best alleviated by ejecting the hostile protagonists from the group
    C. normal and should be handled as such
    D. usually a sign that the agency or worker is lacking in some way
    E. not helpful to the group or worker and, therefore, the best solution is to terminate the meetings until such feelings have subsided

4. To a group worker, the writing of records and reports is   4._____

    A. not necessary but can be a useful aid to his job
    B. an important part of his responsibility
    C. unimportant compared to the more "human" aspects of his job
    D. an uninteresting and unexciting part of his job that must be done
    E. clinical and impersonal, and has no place in the area of true social work

5. Of the following objectives of having children work in committees, the MOST important is to   5._____

    A. develop self-direction in the areas of the social amenities and of parliamentary procedure
    B. improve children's ability in speaking effectively before a group
    C. develop initiative and leadership qualities of the bright children and encourage the shy children

D. make learning a cooperative enterprise in thinking through and solving problems
E. stimulate competition within and between groups which will serve to promote greater interest in the group activity

6. The one of the following which is a device to be used in group dynamics is

   A. metronoscope
   B. opaque projector
   C. diorama
   D. sociogram
   E. group profile

7. The findings of research studies that have contrasted leaders and non-leaders in the same group generally agree that leaders are superior to non-leaders in

   A. making adjustments to new situations
   B. ability to accept criticism
   C. intensity of interests
   D. ability to differentiate right from wrong
   E. intelligence

8. Research in group processes has demonstrated that an individual will accept the attitudes of a group if he

   A. is ambitious
   B. is a passive drifter
   C. makes friends quickly
   D. rebels against authority
   E. strongly desires group membership

9. Boys and girls are generally most inclined toward group experiences with members of their own sex when they are between

   A. 2 and 3 years of age
   B. 4 and 5 years of age
   C. 6 and 10 years of age
   D. 11 and 14 years of age
   E. 15 and 18 years of age

10. Of the following, the unique kind of assistance which group counseling provides for a socially maladjusted client is

    A. the opportunity for the client to identify with a stable adult
    B. the special type of social environment which the counseling group affords the client
    C. the client's growing conviction that he has been "chosen" for the group
    D. a lightened academic load to compensate for the time and energy used in the group
    E. the client's belief that he is a fully accepted member of this group

11. In grouping maladjusted clients for group counseling, the MOST important criterion, of the following, is homogeneity of

    A. intelligence
    B. social maturity
    C. personality deviations
    D. age
    E. sex

12. The acceptance of an individual by an already functioning group will depend MOST upon the

    A. degree of authoritative ability which the individual can demonstrate before the group
    B. contribution the individual can make to realization of the group's goals
    C. influence which the individual enjoys in the community as a whole
    D. ability of the individual to provoke the group to concerted action
    E. extent to which the individual accepts the group's norms of behavior

13. Which one of the following is NOT characteristic of the development of a group?

    A. Emergence of collective goals
    B. Solidification of individual roles within the group structure
    C. Growth of group norms for behavior
    D. Development of a group atmosphere of social climate
    E. Stability of leadership, membership, and group goals

14. "Group Dynamics" means a variety of things to many people. Which of the following is the soundest concept of the term?

    A. The structure of the group
    B. The techniques used in the group situation
    C. The factors making for productivity or failure
    D. The forces operating in the group situation
    E. The processes of response and adjustment

15. The status of an individual in a group is determined, for the most part, by

    A. the possession of those qualities the group deems important
    B. his socio-economic level
    C. his status in other groups of which he is a member
    D. the amount of time and energy he is willing to devote to the purposes of the group
    E. his superior ability in guiding the group in formulating, organizing, and realizing its goals

16. The leader of a group of 12-year-old girls is MOST likely to be superior to the other members of the group in

    A. ability to make friends
    B. appearance
    C. school work
    D. artistic or musical talent
    E. status in other groups to which they belong

17. Of the following, the single characteristic MOST important in determining an individual's status in a group of preadolescent boys is

    A. intelligence   B. physical ability
    C. school marks   D. language development
    E. personality

18. Of the following, the MOST important condition underlying the formation of an out-of-school group of eleven-year-old girls is

    A. coming from the same socio-economic level
    B. showing the same signs of physical development
    C. having the same attitudes and interests
    D. being in the same grade at school
    E. having parents who are close friends and who encourage the formation of the group

19. Recent studies of the productivity of individuals while working as members of a group on a joint project have demonstrated that

    A. larger groups are more productive than smaller groups working on similar tasks
    B. individuals function in much the same way in groups as they do in solitary situations
    C. a group goal is needed to motivate individuals to higher levels of performance
    D. high school pupils work better in groups; college students, as individuals
    E. even when a group goal is sought, individuals will always continue to compete on a personal level

20. UNDERSTANDING GROUP BEHAVIOR OF BOYS AND GIRLS was written by

    A. Helen H. Jennings   B. Ruth Cunningham
    C. Jane Waters   D. Alice V. Crow
    E. Sheldon Glueck

21. In comparison with other members of a group, the leader tends to

    A. hold himself in higher esteem
    B. be less spontaneous
    C. be more desirous of being of service to others
    D. be more willing to accept a low level of performance from members of the group
    E. be more authoritative and less compassionate

22. The individual who emerges as the leader of a group is usually

    A. the person with the highest status but not necessarily the best abilities
    B. superior to the other members of the group in a wide variety of abilities
    C. chosen on the basis of personal qualities rather than ability
    D. the same person, no matter in what activities the group participates
    E. the person who, in the judgment of the group, can best meet the demands of the particular problem

23. The degree of cohesiveness which has been established in a group is MOST likely to be lowered by

    A. unfavorable evaluation of the group by outsiders
    B. favorable evaluation of the group by outsiders
    C. decreasing the amount of interaction in the group
    D. increasing the degree of interaction in the group
    E. altering the membership of the group but increasing the degree of interaction

24. Research has shown that neighborhood gangs tend to be more cohesive than groups of the same age functioning as clubs in more formal youth agencies. This would suggest that

    A. the club is potentially longer-lived than the gang
    B. young people join clubs only if they are not accepted by the gang
    C. clubs will not be able to function adequately in a given neighborhood until some way is found to destroy gangs already in existence
    D. the activities of the gang meet the needs of its members better than those of the club program do
    E. the clubs are dominated by adults, thus limiting the expressiveness of its members

24.____

25. Studies of the cohesiveness of small groups have indicated that the more cohesive a group, the

    A. less likely is it that the group will allow any alteration in its present membership
    B. less likely is it that the group will permit internal disagreement with its objective or goals
    C. less perceptive is the group of its own solidarity
    D. more susceptible is the group to disruption caused by loss of a leader
    E. more willing will the group be to defend itself against external criticism

25.____

KEY (CORRECT ANSWERS)

1. B	11. B
2. B	12. E
3. C	13. B
4. B	14. D
5. D	15. A
6. D	16. A
7. E	17. B
8. C	18. D
9. C	19. C
10. B	20. B

21. A
22. E
23. C
24. D
25. E

TEST 2

DIRECTIONS: Each question or incomplete statement is followed by several suggested answers or completions. Select the one that BEST answers the question or completes the statement. *PRINT THE LETTER OF THE CORRECT ANSWER IN THE SPACE AT THE RIGHT.*

1. Which one of the following statements does NOT describe a function of group prejudice?   1.___

   A. It provides a source of egotistic satisfaction.
   B. It justifies various types of discrimination which are considered to be advantageous to the dominant group.
   C. It provides an outlet for aggressive feelings.
   D. It provides convenient scapegoats.
   E. It excludes most of those who are patently "undesirables" from participation in community activities.

2. The essence of _____ groups is that they are personal, intimate, diffuse, spontaneous, and affective (permeated by emotion).   2.___

   A. tertiary   B. secondary
   C. primary   D. marital
   E. centenary

3. The practice of group psychotherapy basically utilizes the fact that   3.___

   A. people generally tend to prefer group discussion to individually working out a problem
   B. attitudes and other characteristics are often group-formed and group-influenced
   C. private treatment is beyond the income of the average man
   D. fears, hostilities, etc. can be acted out rather than spoken about
   E. it is based on practical life situations, i.e., employment, family problems, etc.

4. The ability of an individual to persist as the leader of a group depends upon the availability of the leader and the   4.___

   A. stability of the group structure
   B. socioeconomic level of the group members
   C. size of the group
   D. sex of the group members
   E. "productiveness" of his efforts

5. Of the following, the MOST important determinant of leadership in pre-adolescent children is the child's   5.___

   A. self-confidence   B. sex
   C. physical attractiveness   D. socio-economic status
   E. intelligence level

6. Research in group processes has demonstrated that an individual will accept the attitudes of a group if he   6.___

   A. is ambitious   B. is a passive drifter
   C. makes friends quickly   D. rebels against authority
   E. is a "follower" rather than a "leader"

56

7. As contrasted with the class in which activities are group controlled, the class dominated by the therapist

   A. provides little opportunity for social learning
   B. shows less mastery of course material
   C. increases client anxiety and frustration
   D. promotes self-understanding and self-direction
   E. discourages clients from developing relationships with their peers

8. Excessive domination of a group of children by an adult leader tends to

   A. prevent the formation of subgroups and cliques
   B. suppress the initiative of the members of the group
   C. increase the cohesiveness of the members of the group
   D. increase the awareness of the group members of group goals
   E. accelerate the rate at which group goals are realized

9. Of the following, the one that is NOT a prerequisite for the spontaneous formation of a stable group from an aggregate of individuals is

   A. motivation in terms of a common objective
   B. communication among the individuals
   C. mutual acceptance among the prospective members of the group
   D. similarity in social class
   E. common allegiance to a cause

10. The degree of cohesiveness that has been established in a group can be increased MOST effectively by

    A. increasing the amount of interaction in the group
    B. modifying the purposes for which the group has been organized
    C. increasing the size of the group
    D. having non-group members criticize the leadership of the group
    E. decreasing the size of the group but making it more heterogeneous

11. Studies of small groups have indicated that the less cohesive the group, the

    A. less permissive will it be of deviations from group standards
    B. less susceptible the group to disruptions caused by loss of a leader
    C. less strongly will it defend itself against external criticism
    D. more it realizes its lack of solidarity
    E. less willing it is to submit to an authoritarian leader

12. Studies of the characteristics of leaders have made it clear that the leader of a group

    A. contributes more to the satisfaction of the needs of the members of the group than any other member
    B. differs from the other members of the group in degree of acceptance of nongroup members
    C. is willing to devote more time and energy to the purpose of the group than any other member
    D. is more concerned with his individual problems than other members of the group
    E. is superior to any other group member in social maturity and mental ability

13. Most of the boys in the seventh grade participate informally in a neighborhood group which has many characteristics of a gang. Mark is clearly the leader, while Terry is his most influential lieutenant; Sig has probably the lowest status in the group while Wally, who lives in the neighborhood, seems to have no part in their activities and no interest in the gang. The boy most likely to change his personal views to coalesce with what he sees as the group norm is

    A. Mark
    B. Terry
    C. Sig
    D. Wally
    E. either Mark or Terry

14. In attempting to make use of the findings of group dynamics in classroom management and learning, which of the following procedures is NOT appropriate?

    A. Creating an atmosphere with minimal anxiety and threat field
    B. Permitting students to make the group's decisions without the possibility of the teacher's overruling these decisions
    C. Encouraging free discussion and questioning in the classroom
    D. Regarding lecture methods as less effective devices for obtaining behavioral changes than discussion methods
    E. Extending the fields of client-therapist planning

15. The MOST important factor conducive to successful group work

    A. is initiative and self-direction on the part of the client
    B. is effective classroom management on the part of the therapist
    C. requires that necessary materials be placed within easy reach of the clients
    D. requires that memoranda to show the sequence of activities to be followed by different groups be written on the blackboard
    E. is effective classroom management by a class-elected leader

16. If group work is to be effective,

    A. there must be more than three groups
    B. the children must receive training in responsibility for their own activities
    C. group duties should not be rotated for long periods of time
    D. the therapist should always select the groups
    E. the groups must be stable and homogeneous

17. In most cases, groups should

    A. be based on the abilities of the client
    B. be based on the interests, abilities and achievements of the client
    C. consist of the same clients for all curriculum areas
    D. be based primarily on the physical limitations of the children
    E. be based on the results of sociometric tests

18. After a group has formed and become a cohesive unit, psychologists have defined four additional stages in its development:
    I.   The group develops its own norms of behavior
    II. The group develops it own "atmosphere"
    III. The status and role of individuals in the group become differentiated
    IV. Collective goals begin to emerge
    The sequence in which these four stages generally appear is

    A. III, I, IV, II
    B. I, II, III, IV
    C. II, IV, III, I
    D. III, IV, I, II
    E. IV, III, I, II

19. In a group guidance lesson, airing prejudices and counter-prejudices will

    A. promote a willingness on the part of the clients to probe more deeply into the topic
    B. lead to constructive action by forcing the client to make a choice
    C. arouse antagonisms that might well have been allowed to be dormant
    D. serve to confuse the client by exposing him to conflicting opinions
    E. lead to hostile feelings between clients with opposing points of view

20. During the past twenty years, there has been considerable research to determine the effectiveness of communication nets in small groups. Two of the simplest of the nets are:

    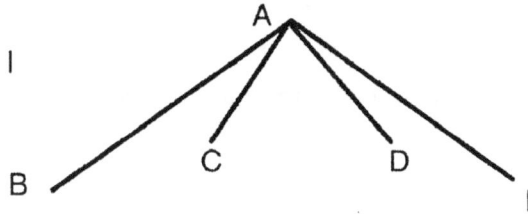
    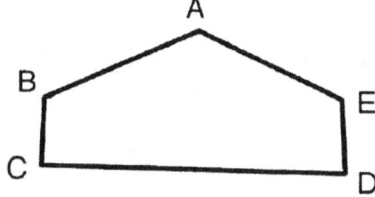

    In each of these, the letter represents an individual and the line a means of two-way communication. The findings, to date, have tended to support the view that the use of network I rather than network II will result in

    A. less enthusiasm among the participants
    B. slower action in solving problems
    C. higher morale in the group as a whole
    D. greater adaptability to change
    E. less flexibility in making administrative decisions

21. For group work to be MOST effective in the teaching of reading in a fourth grade class, the groups should consist of participants who are chosen in terms of their being similar in

    A. emotional age
    B. intelligence quotient
    C. mental age
    D. reading age
    E. chronological age

22. What phase of group therapy *usually* causes the most disequilibrium within the group?

    A. Getting acquainted stage
    B. Minor acting out phase
    C. Major acting out phase
    D. The stage when the group becomes a group
    E. Termination of the group stage

23. Which phase of group therapy is the stage when extreme deviates have been removed and productive activity resumes?

    A. Getting acquainted stage
    B. Minor acting out phase
    C. Crescendo-of-tension phase
    D. The stage when the group becomes a group
    E. Termination of the group stage

24. Which phase of group therapy is the stage of GREATEST equilibrium in which consensus is easily reached and socially deviant behavior is at a minimum?

    A. Getting acquainted stage
    B. Minor acting out phase
    C. Major acting out phase
    D. The stage when the participant becomes a group
    E. Termination of the group stage

25. What information for a situation analysis model approach to the study of psychotherapy groups is included in the area of "setting"? The

    A. nature of the institution and the characteristics of the clientele
    B. emerging interactional patterns among the group members
    C. nature of the conflict as related to the focal event
    D. physical location and intervening aspects of the room
    E. background information that seems significantly related to the focal point

KEY (CORRECT ANSWERS)

1. E	11. C
2. C	12. A
3. B	13. B
4. A	14. B
5. A	15. B
6. C	16. B
7. A	17. B
8. B	18. E
9. D	19. A
10. A	20. A

21. D
22. E
23. C
24. A
25. E

EXAMINATION SECTION
TEST 1

DIRECTIONS: Each question or incomplete statement is followed by several suggested answers or completions. Select the one that BEST answers the question or completes the statement. *PRINT THE LETTER OF THE CORRECT ANSWER IN THE SPACE AT THE RIGHT.*

1. When a counselor is planning a future interview with a client, of the following, the MOST important consideration is the

    A. recommendations he will make to the client
    B. place where the client will be interviewed
    C. purpose for which the client will be interviewed
    D. personality of the client

2. For a counselor to make a practice of reviewing the client's case record, if available, prior to the interview, is, usually,

    A. *inadvisable*, because knowledge of the client's past record will tend to influence the counselor's judgment
    B. *advisable*, because knowledge of the client's background will help the counselor to identify discrepancies in the client's responses
    C. *inadvisable*, because such review is time-consuming and of questionable value
    D. *advisable*, because knowledge of the client's background will help the counselor to understand the client's situation

3. Assume that a counselor makes a practice of constantly reassuring clients with serious and complex problems by making such statements as: "I'm sure you'll soon be well;" "I know you'll get a job soon;" or "Everything will be all right."
   Of the following, the MOST likely result of such a practice is to

    A. encourage the client and make him feel that the counselor understands what the client is going through
    B. make the client doubtful about the counselor's understanding of his difficulties and the counselor's ability to help
    C. confuse the client and cause him to hesitate to take any action on his own initiative
    D. help the client to be more realistic about his situation and the probability that it will improve

4. In order to get the maximum amount of information from a client during an interview, of the following, it is MOST important for the counselor to communicate to the client the feeling that the counselor is

    A. interested in the client
    B. a figure of authority
    C. efficient in his work habits
    D. sympathetic to the client's lifestyle

5. Of the following, the counselor who takes extremely detailed notes during an interview with a client is *most likely* to

    A. encourage the client to talk freely

B. distract and antagonize the client
C. help the client feel at ease
D. understand the client's feelings

6. As a counselor, you find that many of the clients you interview are verbally abusive and unusually hostile to you.
Of the following, the MOST appropriate action for you to take *first* is to

A. review your interviewing techniques and consider whether you may be provoking these clients
B. act in a more authoritative manner when interviewing troublesome clients
C. tell these clients that you will not process their applications unless their troublesome behavior ceases
D. disregard the clients' troublesome behavior during the interview

7. During an interview, you did not completely understand several of your client's responses. In each instance, you rephrased the client's statement and asked the client if that was what he meant.
For you to use such a technique during interviews would be considered

A. *inappropriate;* you may have distorted the client's meaning by rephrasing his statements
B. *inappropriate;* you should have asked the same questioE until you received a comprehensible response
C. *appropriate;* the client will have a chance to correct you if you have misinterpreted his responses
D. *appropriate;* a counselor should rephrase clients' responses for the records

8. A counselor is interviewing a client who has just had a severe emotional shock because of an assault on her by a mugger.
Of the following, the approach which would generally be MOST helpful to the client is for the counselor to

A. comfort the client and encourage her to talk about the assault
B. sympathize with the client but refuse to discuss the assault with her
C. tell the client to control her emotions and think positively about the future
D. proceed with the interview in an impersonal and unemotional manner

9. A counselor finds that her questions are misinterpreted by many of the clients she interviews.
Of the following, the MOST likely reason for this problem is that the

A. client is not listening attentively
B. client wants to avoid the subject being discussed
C. counselor has failed to express her meaning clearly
D. counselor has failed to put the client at ease

10. For a counselor to look directly at the client and observe him during the interview is generally

A. *inadvisable;* this will make the client nervous and uncomfortable
B. *advisable;* the client will be more likely to refrain from lying
C. *inadvisable;* the counselor will not be able to take notes for the case record
D. *advisable;* this will encourage conversation and accelerate the progress of the interview

11. You are interviewing a client who is applying for social services for the first time. In order to encourage this client to freely give you the information needed for you to establish his eligibility, of the following, the BEST way to start the interview is by

    A. asking questions the client can easily answer
    B. conveying the impression that his responses to your questions will be checked
    C. asking two or three similar but important questions
    D. assuring the client that your sole responsibility is "getting the facts"

12. Counselors are encouraged to record significant information obtained from clients and services provided for clients. Of the following, the MOST important reason for this practice is that these case records will

    A. help to reduce the need for regular supervisory conferences
    B. indicate to counselors which clients are taking up the most time
    C. provide information which will help the agency to improve its services to clients
    D. make it easier to verify the complaints of clients

13. As a counselor you find that interviews can be completed in a shorter period of time if you ask questions which limit the client to a certain answer.
    For you to use such a technique would be considered

    A. *inappropriate,* because this type of question usually requires advance preparation
    B. *inappropriate,* because this type of question may inhibit the client from saying what he really means
    C. *appropriate,* because you know the areas into which the questions should be directed
    D. *appropriate,* because this type of question usually helps clients to express themselves clearly

14. Assume that, while you are interviewing an individual to obtain information, the individual pauses in the middle of an answer.
    The BEST of the following actions for you to take at this time is to

    A. correct any inaccuracies in what he has said
    B. remain silent until he continues
    C. explain your position on the matter being discussed
    D. explain that time is short and that he must complete his story quickly

15. You have been assigned to interview the mother of a five-year-old son in her home to get information useful in locating the child's absent father. During the interview, you notice many serious bruises on the child's arms and legs, which the mother explains are due to the child's clumsiness. Of the following, your BEST course of action is to

    A. accept the mother's explanation and concentrate on getting information which will help you to locate the father
    B. advise the mother to have the child examined for a medical condition that may be causing his clumsiness
    C. make a surprise visit to the mother later, to see if someone is beating the child
    D. complete your interview with the mother and report the case to your supervisor for investigation of possible child abuse

16. During an interview, the former landlord of an absent father offers to help you to locate the father if you will give the landlord confidential information you have on the financial situation of the father.
Of the following, you should

    A. immediately end the interview with the landlord
    B. urge the landlord to help you but explain that you are not permitted to give him confidential information
    C. freely give the landlord the confidential information he requests about the father
    D. give the landlord the information only if he promises to keep it confidential

17. You feel that your client, a released mental patient, is not adjusting well to living on his own in an apartment. To gather more information, you interview privately his next-door neighbor, who claims that the client is creating a "disturbance" and speaks of the client in an angry and insulting manner.
Of the following, the BEST action for you to take in this situation is to

    A. listen patiently to the neighbor to try to get the facts about your client's behavior
    B. inform the neighbor that he has no right to speak insultingly about a mentally ill person
    C. make an appointment to interview the neighbor some other time when he isn't so upset
    D. tell the neighbor that you were not aware of the client's behavior and that you will have the client moved

18. As a counselor, you are interviewing a client to determine his eligibility for a work program. Suddenly the client begins to shout that he is in no condition to work and that you are persecuting him for no reason.
Of the following, your BEST response to this client is to

    A. advise the client to stop shouting or you will call for the security guard
    B. wait until the client calms down, then order him to come back for another interview
    C. insist that you are not persecuting the client and that he must complete the interview
    D. wait until the client calms down, say that you understand how he feels, and try to continue the interview

19. You are interviewing a mother whose 17-year-old son has recently been returned home from a mental institution. Although she is willing to care for her son at home, she is frightened by his strange and sometimes violent behavior and does not know the best arrangement to make for his care.
Of the following, your MOST appropriate response to this mother's problem is to

    A. describe the supportive services and alternatives to home care which are available
    B. help her to accept her son's strange and violent behavior
    C. tell her that she will not be permitted to care for her son at home if she is frightened by his behavior
    D. convince her that she is not responsible for her son's mental condition

20. Assume that you are interviewing an elderly man who comes to the center several times a month to discuss topics with you which are not related to social services. You realize that the man is lonely and enjoys these conversations.
    Of the following, it would be MOST appropriate to

    A. politely discourage the man from coming in to pass the time with you
    B. avoid speaking to this man the next time he comes into the center
    C. explore with the client his feelings about joining a senior citizens' center
    D. continue to hold these conversations with the man

21. A client you are interviewing tends to ramble on after each response that he gives, so that many clients are kept waiting.
    In this situation, of the following, it would be MOST advisable to

    A. try to direct the interview, in order to obtain the necessary information
    B. reduce the number of questions asked so that you can shorten the interview
    C. arrange a second interview for the client so that you can give him more time
    D. tell the client that he is wasting everybody's time

22. A non-minority counselor is about to interview a minority client on public assistance for job placement when the client says: "What does your kind know about my problems? You've never had to survive out on these streets."
    Of the following, the counselor's MOST appropriate response in this situation is to

    A. postpone the interview until a minority counselor is available to interview the client
    B. tell the client that he must cooperate with the counselor if he wants to continue receiving public assistance
    C. explain to the client the function of the counselor in this unit and the services he provides
    D. assure the client that you do not have to be a member of a minority group to understand the effects of poverty

23. When you are interviewing someone to obtain information, the BEST of the following reasons for you to repeat certain of his exact words is to

    A. *assure* him that appropriate action will be taken
    B. *encourage* him to elaborate on a point he has made
    C. *assure* him that you agree with his point of view
    D. *encourage* him to switch to another topic of discussion

24. You are interviewing a young client who seriously under-estimates the amount of education and training he will require for a certain occupation.
    For you to tell the client that you think he is mistaken would generally be considered

    A. *inadvisable*, because counselors should not express their opinions to clients
    B. *inadvisable*, because clients have the right to self-determination
    C. *advisable*, because clients should generally be alerted to their misconceptions
    D. *advisable*, because counselors should convince clients to adopt a proper life style

25. Of the following, the MOST appropriate manner for a counselor to assume during an interview with a patient is

    A. authoritarian
    B. paternal
    C. casual
    D. businesslike

KEY (CORRECT ANSWERS)

1. C	11. A
2. D	12. C
3. B	13. B
4. A	14. B
5. B	15. D
6. A	16. B
7. C	17. A
8. A	18. D
9. C	19. A
10. D	20. C

21. A
22. C
23. B
24. C
25. D

TEST 2

DIRECTIONS: Each question or incomplete statement is followed by several suggested answers or completions. Select the one that *BEST* answers the question or completes the statement. *PRINT THE LETTER OF THE CORRECT ANSWER IN THE SPACE AT THE RIGHT.*

1. You are interviewing a legally responsible absent father who refuses to make child support payments because he claims the mother physically abuses the child.
   Of the following, the *BEST* way for you to handle this situation is to tell the father that you

   A. will report his complaint about the mother, but he is still responsible for making child support payments
   B. suspect that he is complaining about the mother in order to avoid his own responsibility for making child support payments
   C. are concerned with his responsibility to make child support payments, not with the mother's abuse of the child
   D. can not determine his responsibility for making child support payments until his complaint about the mother is investigated

2. You are interviewing an elderly woman who lives alone to determine her eligibility for homemaker service at public expense. Though obviously frail and in need of this service, the woman is not completely cooperative, and during the interview, is often silent for a considerable period of time.
   Of the following, the *BEST* way for you to deal with these periods of silence is to

   A. realize that she may be embarrassed to have to apply for homemaker service at public expense, and emphasize her right to this service
   B. postpone the interview and make an appointment with her for a later date, when she may be better able to cooperate
   C. explain to the woman that you have many clients to interview and need her cooperation to complete the interview quickly
   D. recognize that she is probably hiding something and begin to ask questions to draw her out

3. During a conference with an adolescent boy at a juvenile detention center, you find out for the first time that he would prefer to be placed in foster care rather than return to his natural parents.
   To uncover the reasons why the boy dislikes his own home, of the following, it would be *MOST* advisable for you to

   A. ask the boy a number of short, simple questions about his feelings
   B. encourage the boy to talk freely and express his feelings as best he can
   C. interview the parents and find out why the boy doesn't want to live at home
   D. administer a battery of psychological tests in order to make an assessment of the boy's problems

4. You are interviewing a mother who is applying for Aid to Families with Dependent Children because the husband has deserted the family. The mother becomes annoyed at having to answer your questions and tells you to leave her apartment.
   Which one of the following actions would be *most appropriate* to take *FIRST* in this situation?

A. Return to the office and close the case for lack of cooperation
B. Tell the mother that you will get the information from her neighbors if she does not cooperate
C. Tell the mother that you must stay until you get answers to your questions
D. Explain to the mother the reasons for the interview and the consequences of Her failure to cooperate

5. A counselor counseling juvenile clients finds that, although he can tolerate most of their behavior, he becomes infuriated when they lie to him.
Of the following, the counselor can BEST deal with his anger at his clients' lying by

   A. recognizing his feelings of anger and learning to control expression of these feelings to his clients
   B. warning his clients that he cannot be responsible for his anger when a client lies to him
   C. using will power to suppress his feelings of anger when a client lies to him
   D. realizing that lying is a common trait of juveniles and not directed against him personally

6. During an interview, one of your clients, a former drug addict, has expressed an interest in attending a community counseling center and resuming his education.
In this case, the MOST appropriate action that you should take FIRST is to

   A. determine whether this ambition is realistic for a former drug addict
   B. send the client's application to a community counseling center which provides services to former addicts
   C. ask the client whether he is really motivated or is just seeking your approval
   D. encourage and assist the client to take this step, since his interest is a positive sign

7. You are interviewing a client who, during previous appointments, has not responded to your requests for information required to determine his continued eligibility for services. On this occasion, the client again offers an excuse which you feel is not acceptable.
For you to advise the client of the probable loss of services because of his lack of cooperation is

   A. inappropriate, because the threat to withhold services will harm the relationship between counselor and client
   B. inappropriate, because counselors should not reveal to clients that they do not believe their statements
   C. appropriate, because social services are a reward given to cooperative clients
   D. appropriate, because the counselor should Inform clients of the consequences of their lack of cooperation

8. Assume that you are counselling an adolescent boy in a juvenile detention center who has been a ringleader in smuggling "pot" into the center.
During your regular interview with this boy, of the following, it would be advisable to

   A. tell him you know that he has been involved in smuggling pot and that you are trying to understand the reasons for his misbehavior
   B. ignore his pot smuggling in order to reassure him that you understand and accept him, even though you do not agree with his standards of behavior
   C. warn him that you have reported his pot smuggling and that he will be punished for his misbehavior
   D. show him that you disapprove of his pot smuggling, but assure him that you will not report him for his misbehavior

9. Your unit has received several complaints about a homeless elderly woman living outdoors in various locations in the area. To help determine the need for protective services for this woman, you interview several persons in the neighborhood who are familiar with her, but all are uncooperative or reluctant to give information.
Of the following, your BEST approach to these persons is to explain to them that

   A. you will take legal steps against them if they do not cooperate with you
   B. their cooperation may enable you to help this homeless woman
   C. you need their cooperation to remove this homeless woman from their neighborhood
   D. they will be responsible for any harm that comes to this homeless woman

10. Assume that you are interviewing a client regarding an adjustment in budget. The client begins to scream at you that she holds you responsible for the decrease in her allowance.
Of the following, which is the BEST way for you to handle this situation?

   A. Attempt to discuss the matter calmly with the client and explain her right to a hearing
   B. Urge the client to appeal and assure her of your support
   C. Tell the client that her disorderly behavior will be held against her
   D. Tell the client that the reduction is "due to red tape" and is not your fault

11. As a counselor assigned to a juvenile detention center, you are having a counselling interview with a recently admitted boy who is having serious problems in adjusting to confinement in the center. During the interview, the boy frequently interrupts to ask you personal questions. Of the following, the BEST way for you to deal with these questions is to

   A. tell him in a friendly way that your job is to discuss his problems, not yours
   B. try to understand how the questions relate to the boy's own problems and reply with discretion
   C. take no notice of the questions and continue with the interview
   D. try to win the boy's confidence by answering his questions in detail

12. A counselor is interviewing an elderly woman who hesitates to provide necessary information about her finances to determine whether she is eligible for supplementary assistance. She fears that this information will be reported to others and that her neighbors will find out that she is destitute and applying for "welfare." Of the following, the counselor's MOST appropriate response is to

   A. tell her that, if she hesitates to give this information, the agency will get it from other sources
   B. assure her that this information is kept strictly confidential and will not be given to unauthorized persons
   C. convince her that her application will be turned down unless she provides this information as soon as possible
   D. ask for the name and address of her nearest relative and obtain the information from that person

13. You are counseling a couple whose children have been placed in a foster home because of the couple's quarreling and child neglect. When you interview the wife by herself, she tells you that she knows the husband often "cheats" on her with other women, but she is too afraid of the husband's temper to tell him how much this hurts her.
For you to immediately reveal to the husband the wife's unhappiness concerning his "cheating" is, generally,

    A. *good practice,* because it will help the husband to understand why his wife quarrels with him
    B. *poor practice,* because information received from the wife should not be given to the husband without her permission
    C. *good practice,* because the husband will direct his anger at you rather than at his wife
    D. poor *practice,* because the wife may have told you a false story about her husband in order to win your sympathy

14. A counselor is beginning a job placement interview with a tall, strongly built young man. As the man sits down, the counselor comments: "I know a big fellow like you wouldn't be interested in any clerical job."
For the counselor to make such a comment is, generally,

    A. *appropriate,* because it creates an air of familiarity which may put the man at ease
    B. *inappropriate,* because the man may be sensitive about his physical size
    C. *appropriate,* because, the counselor is using his judgment to help speed up the interview
    D. *inappropriate,* because the man may feel he is being pressured into agreeing with the counselor

15. A counselor in a men's shelter is counseling a middle-aged client for alcoholism. During counseling, the" client confesses that, many years ago, he had often enjoyed sexually abusing his ten-year-old daughter. The counselor tells the client that he personally finds the client's behavior "morally disgusting."
For the counselor to tell the client this is, generally,

    A. *acceptable counseling practice,* because it may encourage the client to feel guilty about his behavior
    B. un*acceptable* cou*seling practice* , because the client may try to shock the counselor by confessing other similar behavior
    C. *acceptable counseling practice,* because "letting off steam" in this manner may relieve tension between the counselor and the client
    D. *unacceptable counseling practice,* because the client may hesitate to discuss his behavior frankly with the counselor in the future

16. During an interview, your client, who wants to move to a larger apartment, asks you to decide on a suitable neighborhood for her.
    For you to make such a decision for the client would, generally, be considered

    A. *appropriate,* because you can save time and expense by sharing your knowledge of neighborhoods with the client
    B. *inappropriate,* because counselors should not help clients with this type of decision
    C. *appropriate,* because this will help the client to develop confidence in her ability to make decisions
    D. *inappropriate,* because the client should be encouraged to accept the responsibility of making this decision

17. A client tells you that he is extremely upset by the treatment that he received from Center personnel at the information desk.
    Which of the following is the *BEST* way to handle this complaint during the interview?

    A. Explain to the client that he probably misinterpreted what occurred at the information desk
    B. Let the client express his feelings and then proceed with the interview
    C. Tell the client that you are not concerned with the personnel at the information desk
    D. Escort the client to the information desk to find out what really happened

18. You are finishing an interview with a client in which you have explained to her the procedure she must go through to apply for income maintenance.
    Of the following, the *BEST* way for you to make sure that she has fully understood the procedure is to ask her

    A. whether she feels she has understood your explanation of the procedure
    B. whether she has any questions to ask you about the procedure
    C. to describe the procedure to you in her own words
    D. a few questions to test her understanding of the procedure

19. You are interviewing a client in his home as part of your investigation of an anonymous complaint that he has been receiving Medicaid fraudulently. During the interview, the client frequently interrupts your questions to discuss the hardships of his life and the bitterness he feels about his medical condition.
    Of the following, the *BEST* way for you to deal with these discussions is to

    A. cut them off abruptly, since the client is probably just trying to avoid answering your questions
    B. listen patiently, since these discussions may be helpful to the client and may give you information for your investigation
    C. remind the client that you are investigating a complaint against him and he must answer directly
    D. seek to gain the client's confidence by discussing any personal or medical problems which you yourself may have

20. While interviewing an absent father to determine his ability to pay child supprt, you realize that his answers to some of your questions contradict his answers to other questions. Of the following, the BEST way for you to try to get accurate information from the father is to

    A. confront him with his contradictory answers and demand an explanation from him
    B. use your best judgment as to which of his answers are accurate and question him accordingly
    C. tell him that he has misunderstood your questions and that he must clarify his answers
    D. ask him the same questions in different words and follow up his answers with related questions

21. The one of the following types of interviewees who presents the LEAST difficult problem to handle is the person who

    A. answers with a great many qualifications
    B. talks at length about unrelated subjects so that the counselor cannot ask questions
    C. has difficulty understanding the counselor's vocabulary
    D. breaks into the middle of sentences and completes them with a meaning of his own

22. A man being interviewed is entitled to Medicaid, but he refuses to sign up for it because he says he cannot accept any form of welfare.
    Of the following, the BEST course of action to take FIRST is to

    A. try to discover the reason for his feeling this way
    B. tell him that he should be glad financial help is available
    C. explain that others cannot help him if he will not help himself
    D. suggest that he speak to someone who is already on Medicaid

23. Of the following, the outcome of an interview by a counselor depends MOST heavily on the

    A. personality of the interviewee
    B. personality of the counselor
    C. subject matter of the questions asked
    D. interaction between counselor and interviewee.

24. Some clients being interviewed are primarily interested in making a favorable impression. The counselor should be aware of the fact that such clients are *more likely* than other clients to

    A. try to anticipate the answers the interviewer is looking for
    B. answer all questions openly and frankly
    C. try to assume the role of interviewer
    D. be anxious to get the interview over as quickly as possible

25. The type of interview which a counselor usually conducts is substantially different from most interviewing situations in all of the following aspects EXCEPT the

    A. setting
    B. kinds of clients
    C. techniques employed
    D. kinds of problems

KEY (CORRECT ANSWERS)

1.	A	11.	B
2.	A	12.	B
3.	B	13.	B
4.	D	14.	D
5.	A	15.	D
6.	D	16.	D
7.	D	17.	B
8.	A	18.	C
9.	B	19.	B
10.	A	20.	D

21. C
22. A
23. D
24. A
25. C

EXAMINATION SECTION
TEST 1

DIRECTIONS: Each question or incomplete statement is followed by several suggested answers or completions. Select the one that BEST answers the question or completes the statement. *PRINT THE LETTER OF THE CORRECT ANSWER IN THE SPACE AT THE RIGHT.*

1. It is generally accepted that, of the following, the MOST important medium for developing integration and continuity in learning on the job is
   A. day-to-day experience on the job
   B. the supervisory conference
   C. the staff meeting
   D. the professional seminar

   1.____

2. Assume that you find that one of your workers is over-identifying with a particular client.
   Of the following, the MOST appropriate step for you to take FIRST in dealing with this situation is to
   A. transfer the cases to another worker
   B. inform the worker that he cannot give satisfactory service if he over-identifies with a client
   C. interview the client yourself to determine his feelings about his relationship with the worker
   D. arrange a conference with the worker to discuss the reasons for her over-identification with this client

   2.____

3. The one of the following which is the MOST likely reason why a newly-appointed supervisor would have a tendency to interfere actively in a relationship between one of his workers and a client is that the supervisor
   A. has unresolved feelings about relinquishing the role of worker, and has not yet accepted his role as supervisor
   B. must give direct assistance in the situation because the worker cannot handle it
   C. is attempting to share with his worker the knowledge and skill which he has developed in direct practice
   D. has not realized that immediate responsibility for work with clients has been delegated to others

   3.____

4. A worker who has a tendency to resist authority and supervision can be helped MOST effectively if, of the following, the supervisor
   A. behaves in a strict and impersonal manner so that the worker will accept his authority as a supervisor
   B. modifies the relationship so that he will be less authoritarian and threatening to the worker
   C. gives the worker a simple, matter-of-fact interpretation of the supervisory relationship and has an understanding acceptance of the worker's response
   D. temporarily establishes a peer relationship with the worker in order to overcome his resistance

   4.____

5. Before interviewing a newly-appointed worker for the first time, of the following, it is DESIRABLE for the supervisor to
   A. learn as much as he can about the worker's background and interests in order to eliminate the routine of asking questions and eliciting answers
   B. review the job information to be covered in order to make it easier to be impersonal and keep to the business at hand
   C. send the worker orientation material about the agency and the job and ask him to study it before the interview
   D. review available information about the worker in order to find an area of shared experience to serve as a *taking off* point for getting acquainted

6. In interviewing a new worker, of the following, it is IMPORTANT for the supervisor to
   A. give direction to the progress of the interview and maintain a leadership role throughout
   B. allow the worker to take the initiative in order to give him full scope for freedom of expression
   C. maintain a non-directional approach so that the worker will reveal his true attitudes and feelings
   D. avoid interrupting the worker, even though he seems to want to do all the talking

7. When a new worker, during his first few days, shows such symptoms of insecurity as *stage fright*, helpless immobility, or extreme talkativeness, of the following, it would be MOST helpful for the supervisor to
   A. start the worker out on some activity in which he is relatively secure
   B. ignore the symptoms and allow the worker to *sink or swim* on his own
   C. have a conference with the worker and interpret to him the reasons for his feelings of insecurity
   D. consider the probability that this worker may not be suited for a profession which requires skill in interpersonal relationships

8. Of the following, the MOST desirable method of minimizing workers' dependence on the supervisor and encouraging self-dependence is to
   A. hold group instead of individual supervisory conferences at regular intervals
   B. schedule individual supervisory conferences only in response to the workers' obvious need for guidance
   C. plan for progressive exposure to other opportunities for learning afforded by the agency and the community
   D. allow workers to learn by trial and error rather than by direct supervisory guidance

9. Of the following, it would NOT be appropriate for the supervisor to use early supervisory conferences with the new workers as a means of
   A. giving him direct practical help in order to get going on the job
   B. estimating the level of his native abilities, professional skills and experience
   C. getting clues as to his characteristic ways of learning in a new situation
   D. assessing his potential for future supervisory responsibility

10. Without careful planning by the supervisor for orientation of the new worker, an informal system of orientation by co-workers inevitably develops.
Such an informal system of orientation is USUALLY
   A. *beneficial*, because many new workers learn more readily when instructed by their peers
   B. *harmful*, because informal orientation by an undesignated co-worker can lead a new worker astray instead of helping him
   C. *beneficial*, because assumption by subordinates of responsibility for orientation will free the supervisor for other urgent work
   D. *harmful*, because such informal orientation by a co-worker will tend to destroy the authority of the supervisor

11. Of the following, the BEST way for a supervisor to assist a subordinate who has unusual work pressures is to
   A. relieve him of some of his cases until the pressures subside
   B. help him to decide which cases should be given the most attention during the period of pressure, and how to provide coverage for less urgent cases
   C. inform him that he must learn to tolerate and adjust to such pressures
   D. point out that he should learn to understand the causes of the pressures, which probably resulted from his own deficiencies

12. Many supervisors have a tendency to use case records mainly for the purpose of analysis of the workers' skill or evaluation of their performance.
Of the following, a PROBABLE result of this practice is that
   A. workers are likely to tie-in recording with supervisory evaluation of their work, without giving proper emphasis to their importance in improving service to clients
   B. the worker is likely to devote an inordinate amount of time to case records at the expense of his clients
   C. the records are likely to be too lengthy and detailed, limiting their value for other important purposes
   D. the records are likely to be of little value for administrative and research purposes

13. A common obstacle to adequate recording in a large social work agency is the fact that many workers consider recording to be a time-consuming chore.
In order to obtain the cooperation of staff in keeping proper records, of the following, it is MOST important for an agency to provide
   A. indisputable evidence of the intelligent use of records as tools in formulating policy and improving service
   B. a system of checks and controls to assure that workers are preparing adequate and timely records
   C. adequate clerical services and mechanical equipment for recording
   D. sufficient time for recording in the organization of every job

14. The one of the following which is NOT a purpose of keeping case records in an agency is
   A. planning
   B. research
   C. training
   D. job classification

15. When a supervisor is reviewing the records of a worker, of the following, he should plan to read
   A. records of new cases only, following up each interview selectively
   B. the total caseload, in order to determine which aspects of the worker's performance should be examined
   C. those records which the worker has brought to the supervisor's attention because of the need for help
   D. a block of records selected according to the worker's need for help, and some records selected at random

15.____

16. The one of the following which is the PRIMARY purpose of the regular staff meeting in an agency is
   A. initiation of action in order to get the agency's work done
   B. staff training and development
   C. program and policy determination
   D. communication of new policies and procedures

16.____

17. Of the following, group supervision in an agency is intended as a means of
   A. strengthening the total supervisory process
   B. shifting the focus of supervision from the individual to the group
   C. saving costs in terms of time and manpower
   D. influencing policy through group interaction

17.____

18. The supervisor's job brings him closer to such limiting factors in the operation of an agency as faulty administrative structure, shortage of funds and lack of facilities, inadequacies in personnel practices, community pressures, and excessive workload.
For the supervisor to make a practice of communicating to his subordinates his feelings of frustration about such limitations in the work setting would be
   A. *appropriate*, because the worker will be more understanding of the supervisor's burdens and frustrations
   B. *inappropriate*, because the climate created will block rather than further the purposes of supervision
   C. *appropriate*, because such communication will create a more democratic climate between the worker and the supervisor
   D. *inappropriate*, because the supervisor must support and condone agency policies and practices in the presence of subordinates

18.____

19. A suggestion has been made that the teaching and administrative functions of supervision should be separated, so that the supervisor responsible for teaching would not be responsible for evaluation of the same workers.
The one of the following which is the MOST important reason for this point of view is that
   A. elements that confer on the supervisor a position of authority and power unduly threaten the learning situation
   B. teaching skill and administrative ability do not usually go together

19.____

C. a supervisor who has been responsible for training a worker is likely to be prejudiced in his favor
D. performance evaluation and total job accountability should be two separate functions

20. In reviewing a worker's cases in preparation for a periodic evaluation, you note that she has done a uniformly good job with certain types of cases and poor work with other types of cases.
Of the following, the BEST approach for you to take in this situation is to
   A. bring this to the worker's attention, find out why she favors certain types of clients, and discuss ways in which she can improve her service to all clients
   B. bring this to the worker's attention and suggest that she may need professional counseling, as she seems to be blocked in working with certain types of cases
   C. assign to her mainly those cases which she handles best and transfer the types of cases which she handles poorly to another worker
   D. accept the fact that a worker cannot be expected to give uniformly good service to all clients, and take no further action

KEY (CORRECT ANSWERS)

1.	B	11.	B
2.	D	12.	A
3.	A	13.	A
4.	C	14.	D
5.	D	15.	D
6.	A	16.	A
7.	A	17.	A
8.	C	18.	B
9.	D	19.	A
10.	B	20.	A

TEST 2

DIRECTIONS: Each question or incomplete statement is followed by several suggested answers or completions. Select the one that BEST answers the question or completes the statement. *PRINT THE LETTER OF THE CORRECT ANSWER IN THE SPACE AT THE RIGHT.*

1. Of the following, the choice of method to be used in the supervisory process should be influenced MOST by the
    A. number and type of cases carried by each worker
    B. emotional maturity of the worker
    C. number of workers supervised and their past experience
    D. subject matter to be learned and the long-range goals of supervision

    1.____

2. In an evaluation conference with a worker, the BEST approach for the supervisor to take is to
    A. help the worker to identify his strengths as a basis for working on his weaknesses
    B. identify the worker's weaknesses and help him overcome them
    C. allow the worker to identify his weaknesses first and then suggest ways of overcoming them
    D. discuss the worker's weaknesses but emphasize his strengths

    2.____

3. Assume that a worker is discouraged about the progress of his work and feels that it is futile to attempt to cope with many of his cases.
   Of the following, it would be BEST for the supervisor to
    A. suggest to the worker that such feelings are inappropriate for a professional worker
    B. tell the worker that he must seek professional help in order to overcome these feelings
    C. reduce the worker's caseload and give him cases that are less complex
    D. review with the worker several of his cases in which there were obvious accomplishments

    3.____

4. The supervisor is responsible for providing the worker with the following means of support, with the EXCEPTION of
    A. interest and advice on his personal problems
    B. instruction on community resources
    C. inspiration for carrying out the work of the agency
    D. understanding his strengths and limitations

    4.____

5. When a worker frequently takes the initiative in asking questions and discussing problems during a supervisory conference, this is PROBABLY an indication that the
    A. supervisor is not sufficiently interested in the work
    B. conference is a positive learning experience for the worker
    C. worker is hostile and resists supervision
    D. supervisor's position of authority is in question

    5.____

6. When a supervisor finds that one of his workers cannot accept criticism, of the following, it would be BEST for the supervisor to
   A. have the worker transferred to another supervisor
   B. warn the worker of disciplinary proceedings unless his attitude changes
   C. have the worker suspended after explaining the reason
   D. explore with the worker his attitude toward authority

7. Of the following, the condition which the inexperienced worker is LEAST likely to be aware of, without the guidance of the supervisor, is
   A. when he is successful in helping a client
   B. when he is not making progress in helping a client
   C. that he has a personal bias toward certain clients
   D. that he feels insecure because of lack of experience

8. The supervisor should provide an inexperienced worker with controls as well as freedom MAINLY because controls will
   A. enable him to set up his own controls sooner
   B. put him in a situation which is closer to the realities of life
   C. help him to use authority in handling a casework problem
   D. give him a feeling of security and lay the foundation for future self-direction

9. A result of the use of summarized case recording by the worker is that it
   A. gives the supervisor more responsibility for selecting cases to discuss in conference
   B. makes more time available for other activities
   C. lowers the morale of many workers
   D. decreases discussion of cases by the worker and the supervisor

10. The distinction between the role of professional workers and the role of auxiliary or sub-professional workers in an agency is based upon the
    A. position within the agency hierarchy
    B. amount of close supervision given
    C. emergent nature of tasks assigned
    D. functions performed

11. Of the following, the MOST important source of learning for the worker should be
    A. departmental directives and professional literature
    B. his co-workers in the agency
    C. the content of in-service training courses
    D. the clients in his caseload

12. A client is MOST likely to feel that he is receiving acceptance and understanding if the social worker
    A. gets detailed information about the client's problem
    B. demonstrates that he realistically understands the client's problem
    C. has an intellectual understanding of the client's problem
    D. offers the client assurance of assistance

13. A client will be MORE encouraged to speak freely about his problems if the worker
    A. avoids asking too many questions
    B. asks leading rather than pointed questions
    C. suggests possible answers
    D. identifies with the client

14. A client would be MOST likely to be able to accept help in a time of crisis and need if the worker
    A. explains agency policy to him
    B. responds immediately to the client's need
    C. explains why help cannot be given immediately
    D. reaches out to help the client establish his rightful claim for assistance

15. It is a generally accepted principle that the worker should interpret for himself what the client is saying, but usually should not pass his interpretation on to the client because the client
    A. will become hostile to the worker
    B. should arrive at his own conclusions at his own pace
    C. must request the interpretation first
    D. usually wants facts, rather than the worker's interpretation

16. In evaluating the client's capacity to cope with his problems, it is MOST important for the worker to assess his ability to
    A. form close relationships
    B. ask for help
    C. express his hostility
    D. verbalize his difficulties

17. When a worker finds that he disagrees strongly with an agency policy, it is DESIRABLE for him to
    A. share his feelings about the policy with his client
    B. understand fully why he has such strong feelings about the policy
    C. refer cases involving the policy to his supervisor
    D. refuse to give help in cases involving the policy

18. Which of the following practices is BEST for a supervisor to use when assigning work to his staff?
    A. Give workers with seniority the most difficult jobs
    B. Assign all unimportant work to the slower workers
    C. Permit each employee to pick the job he prefers
    D. Make assignments based on the workers' abilities

19. In which of the following instances is a supervisor MOST justified in giving commands to people under his supervision?
    When
    A. they delay in following instructions which have been given to them clearly
    B. they become relaxed and slow about work, and he wants to speed up their production
    C. he must direct them in an emergency situation
    D. he is instructing them on jobs that are unfamiliar to them

20. Which of the following supervisory actions or attitudes is MOST likely to result in getting subordinates to try to do as much work as possible for a supervisor?
He
   A. shows that his most important interest is in schedules and production goals
   B. consistently pressures his staff to get the work out
   C. never fails to let them know he is in charge
   D. considers their abilities and needs while requiring that production goals be met

20.____

KEY (CORRECT ANSWERS)

1.	D	11.	D
2.	A	12.	B
3.	D	13.	D
4.	A	14.	D
5.	B	15.	B
6.	D	16.	A
7.	C	17.	B
8.	D	18.	D
9.	B	19.	C
10.	D	20.	D

TEST 3

DIRECTIONS: Each question or incomplete statement is followed by several suggested answers or completions. Select the one that BEST answers the question or completes the statement. *PRINT THE LETTER OF THE CORRECT ANSWER IN THE SPACE AT THE RIGHT.*

1. One of your workers comes to you and complains in an angry manner about your having chosen him for some particular assignment. In your opinion, the subject of the complaint is trivial land unimportant, but it seems to be quite important to your worker.
   The BEST of the following actions for you to take in this situation is to
   A. allow the worker to continue talking until he has calmed down and then explain the reasons for your having chosen him for that particular assignment
   B. warn the worker to moderate his tone of voice at once because he is bordering on insubordination
   C. tell the worker in a friendly tone that he is making a tremendous fuss over an extremely minor matter
   D. point out to the worker that you are his immediate supervisor and that you are running the unit in accordance with official policy

   1.____

2. The one of the following which is the LEAST desirable action for an assistant supervisor to take in disciplining a subordinate for an infraction of the rules is to
   A. caution him against repetition of the infraction, even if it is minor
   B. point out his progress in applying the rules at the same time that you reprimand him
   C. be as specific as possible in reprimanding him for rule infractions
   D. allow a cooling-off period to elapse before reprimanding him

   2.____

3. A training program for workers assigned to the intake section should include actual practice in simulated interviews under simulated conditions.
   The one of the following educational principles which is the CHIEF justification for this statement is that
   A. the workers will remember what they see better and longer than what they read or hear
   B. the workers will learn more effectively by actually doing the act themselves than they would learn from watching others do it
   C. the conduct of simulated interviews once or twice will enable them to cope with the real situation with little difficulty
   D. a training program must employ methods of a practical nature if the workers are to find anything of lasting value in it

   3.____

4. In order for a supervisor to employ the system of democratic leadership in his supervision, it would generally be BEST for him to
   A. allow his subordinates to assist in deciding on methods of work performance and job assignments but only in those areas where decisions have not been made on higher administrative levels

   4.____

B. allow his subordinates to decide how to do the required work, interposing his authority when work is not completed on schedule or is improperly completed
C. attempt to make assignments of work to individuals only of the type which they enjoy doing
D. maintain control over job assignment and work production, but allow the subordinates to select methods of work and internal conditions of work at democratically conducted staff conferences

5. In a unit in which supervision has been considered quite effective, it has become necessary to press for above-normal production for a limited period to achieve a required goal.
The one of the following which is a LEAST likely result of this pressure is that
   A. there will be more *griping* by employees
   B. some workers will do both more and better work than has been normal for them
   C. there will be an enhanced feeling of group unity
   D. there will be increased absenteeism

6. For a supervisor to encourage competitive feelings among his staff is
   A. *advisable*, chiefly because the workers will perform more efficiently when they have proper motivation
   B. *inadvisable*, chiefly because the workers will not perform well under the pressure of competition
   C. *advisable*, chiefly because the workers will have a greater incentive to perform their job properly
   D. *inadvisable*, chiefly because the workers may focus their attention on areas where they excel and neglect other essential aspects of the job

7. In selecting jobs to be assigned to a new worker, the supervisor should assign those jobs which
   A. give the worker the greatest variety of experience
   B. offer the worker the greatest opportunity to achieve concrete results
   C. present the worker with the greatest stimulation because of their interesting nature
   D. require the least amount of contact with outside agencies

8. A supervisor should avoid a detailed discussion of a worker-client interview with a new worker before the worker has fully recorded the interview CHIEFLY because such a discussion might
   A. cover matters which are already fully covered and explained in the written record
   B. make the worker forget some important deal learned during the interview
   C. color the recording according to the worker's reaction to his supervisor's opinions
   D. minimize the worker's feeling of having reached a decision independently

9. Some supervisors encourage their worker to submit a list of their questions about specific jobs or their comments about problems they wish to discuss in advance of the worker-supervisor conference.
   This practice is
   A. *desirable*, chiefly because it helps to stimulate and focus the worker's thinking about his caseload
   B. *undesirable*, chiefly because it will stifle the worker's free expression of his problems and attitudes
   C. *desirable*, chiefly because it will allow the conference to move along more smoothly and quickly
   D. *undesirable*, chiefly because it will restrict the scope of the conference and the variety of jobs discussed

10. An alert supervisor hears a worker apparently giving the wrong information to a client and immediately reprimands him severely.
    For the supervisor to reprimand the worker at his point is poor CHIEFLY because
    A. instruction must precede correct performance
    B. oral reprimands are less effective than written reprimands
    C. the worker was given no opportunity to explain his reasons for what he did
    D. more effective training can be obtained by discussing the errors with a group of workers

11. The one of the following circumstances when it would generally be MOST proper for a supervisor to do a job himself rather than to train a subordinate to do the job is when it is
    A. a job which the supervisor enjoys doing and does well
    B. not a very time-consuming job but an important one
    C. difficult to train another to do the job, yet is not difficult for the supervisor to do
    D. unlikely that this or any similar job will have to be done again at any future time

12. Effective training of subordinates requires that the supervisor understand certain facts about learning and forgetting processes.
    Among these is the fact that people GENERALLY
    A. forget what they learned at a much greater rate during the first day than during subsequent periods
    B. both learn and forget at a relatively constant rate and this rate is dependent upon their general intellectual capacity
    C. learn at a relatively constant rate except for periods of assimilation when the quantity of retained learning decreases while information is becoming firmly fixed in the mind
    D. learn very slowly at first when introduced to a new topic, after which there is a great increase in the rate of learning

13. It has been suggested that a subordinate who likes his superior will tend to do better work than one who does not.
    According to the MOST widely held current theories of supervision, this suggestion is a
    A. *bad* one, since personal relationships tend to interfere with proper professional relationships
    B. *bad* one, since the strongest motivating factors are fear and uncertainty
    C. *good* one, since liking one's superior is a motivating factor for good work performance
    D. *good* one, since liking one's supervisor is the most important factor in employee performance

14. One factor which might be given consideration in deciding upon the optimum span of control of a supervisor over his immediate subordinates is the position of the supervisor in the hierarchy of the organization.
    It is generally considered proper that the number of subordinates immediately supervised by a higher, upper echelon supervisor _____ the number supervised by lower level supervisors.
    A. is unrelated to and tends to form no pattern with
    B. should be about the same as
    C. should be larger than
    D. should be smaller than

15. The one of the following instances when it is MOST important for an upper level supervisor to follow the chain of command is when he is
    A. communicating decisions   B. communicating information
    C. receiving suggestions   D. seeking information

16. At the end of his probationary period, a supervisor should be considered potentially valuable in his position if he shows
    A. awareness of his areas of strength and weakness, identification with the administration of the department, and ability to learn under supervision
    B. skill in work, supervision, and administration, and a friendly democratic approach to the staff
    C. knowledge of departmental policies and procedures and ability to carry them out, ability to use authority, and ability to direct the work of the staff
    D. an identification with the department, acceptance of responsibility, and ability to give help to the individuals who are to be supervised

17. Good supervision is selective because
    A. it is not necessary to direct all the activities of the person
    B. a supervisor would never have time to know the whole caseload of a worker
    C. workers resent too much help from a supervisor
    D. too much reading is a waste of valuable time

18. An important administrative problem is how precisely to define the limits of authority that is delegated to subordinate supervisors.
Such definition of limits of authority should be
    A. as precise as possible and practicable in all areas
    B. as precise as possible and practicable in areas of function, but should allow considerable flexibility in the area of personnel management
    C. as precise as possible and practicable in the area
    D. of personnel management, but should allow considerable flexibility in the areas of function
    E. in general terms so as to allow considerable flexibility both in the areas of function and in the areas of personnel management

18.____

19. Experts in the field of personnel relations feel that it is generally a bad practice for subordinate employees to become aware of pending or contemplated changes in policy or organizational set-up via the *grapevine* CHIEFLY because
    A. evidence that one or more responsible officials have proved untrustworthy will undermine confidence in the agency
    B. the information disseminated by this method is seldom entirely accurate and generally spreads needless unrest among the subordinate staff
    C. the subordinate staff may conclude that the administration feels the staff cannot be trusted with the true information
    D. the subordinate staff may conclude that the administration lacks the courage to make an unpopular announcement through official channels

19.____

20. Supervision is subject to many interpretations, depending on the area in which it functions.
Of the following, the statement which represents the MOST appropriate meaning of supervision as it is known in social work practice is that it
    A. is a leadership process for the development of new leaders
    B. is an educational and administrative process aimed at teaching personnel the goal of improved service to the client
    C. is an activity aimed chiefly at insuring that workers will adhere to all agency directives
    D. provides the opportunity for administration to secure staff reaction to agency policies

20.____

21. A supervisor may utilize various methods in the supervisory process.
The one of the following upon which sound supervisory practice rests in the selection of supervisory techniques is
    A. an estimate of the worker arrived at through current and past evaluation of performance as well as through worker's participation
    B. the previous supervisor's evaluation and recommendation
    C. the worker's expression of his personal preference for certain types of experience
    D. the amount of time available to supervisor and supervisee

21.____

22. It is the practice of some supervisors, when they believe that it would be desirable for a subordinate to take a particular action in a case, to inform the subordinate of this in the form of a suggestion rather than in the form of a direct order.
In general, this method of getting a subordinate to take the desired action is
    A. *inadvisable*; it may create in the mind of the subordinate the impression that the supervisor is uncertain about the efficacy of her plan and is trying to avoid whatever responsibility she may have in resolving the case
    B. *advisable*; it provides the subordinate with the maximum opportunity to use her own judgment in handling the case
    C. *inadvisable*; it provides the subordinate with no clear-cut direction and, therefore, is likely to leave her with a feeling of uncertainty and frustration
    D. *advisable*; it presents the supervisor's view in a manner which will be most likely to evoke the subordinate's cooperation

23. A veteran supervisor noticed that one of her workers of average ability had begun developing some bad work habits, becoming especially careless in her recordkeeping. After reprimand from the supervisor, the investigator corrected her errors and has been doing satisfactory work since then.
For the supervisor to keep referring to this period of poor work during her weekly conferences with this employee would generally be considered poor personnel practice CHIEFLY because
    A. praise rather than criticism is generally the best method to use in improving the work of an unsatisfactory worker
    B. the supervisor cannot know whether the employee's errors will follow an established pattern
    C. the fault which evoked the original negative criticism no longer exists
    D. this would tend to frustrate the worker by making her strive overly hard to reach a level of productivity which is beyond her ability to achieve

24. Assume that you are now a supervisor in a specific unit. Two experienced investigators in your unit, both of whom do above average work, have for some time not gotten along with each other for personal reasons Their attitude toward one another has suddenly become hostile and noisy disagreement has taken place in the office.
The BEST action for you to take FIRST in this situation is to
    A. transfer one of the two investigators to another unit where contact with the other investigator will be unnecessary
    B. discuss the problem with the two investigators together, insisting that they confide in you and tell you the cause of their mutual antagonism
    C. confer with the two investigators separately, pointing out to each the need to adopt an adult professional attitude with respect to their on-the-job relations
    D. advise the two investigators that should the situation grow worse, disciplinary action will be considered

25. It has long been recognized that relationships exist between worker morale and working conditions.
The one of the following which BEST clarifies these existing relationships is that morale is
   A. affected for better or worse in direct relationship to the magnitude of the changes in working conditions for better or worse
   B. better when working conditions are better
   C. little affected by working conditions so long as the working conditions do not approach the intolerable
   D. more affected by the degree of interest shown in providing good working conditions than by the actual conditions and may, perversely, be highest when working conditions are worst

KEY (CORRECT ANSWERS)

1.	A		11.	D
2.	D		12.	A
3.	B		13.	C
4.	A		14.	D
5.	D		15.	A
6.	D		16.	D
7.	B		17.	A
8.	C		18.	A
9.	A		19.	B
10.	C		20.	B

21. A
22. D
23. C
24. C
25. D

PREPARING WRITTEN MATERIALS
EXAMINATION SECTION
TEST 1

DIRECTIONS: Each question consists of a sentence which may be classified appropriately under one of the following four categories:
  A. Incorrect because of faulty grammar or sentence structure.
  B. Incorrect because of faulty punctuation.
  C. Incorrect because of faulty spelling or capitalization.
  D. Correct

Examine each sentence carefully. Then, in the space at the right, print the capital letter preceding the option which is the BEST of the four suggested above. All incorrect sentences contain only one type of error. Consider a sentence correct if it contains none of the types of errors mentioned, although there may be other correct ways of expressing the same thought.

1. The fire apparently started in the storeroom, which is usually locked. 1.____
2. On approaching the victim two bruises were noticed by this officer. 2.____
3. The officer, who was there examined the report with great care. 3.____
4. Each employee in the office had a separate desk. 4.____
5. The suggested procedure is similar to the one now in use. 5.____
6. No one was more pleased with the new procedure than the chauffeur. 6.____
7. He tried to pursuade her to change the procedure. 7.____
8. The total of the expenses charged to petty cash were high. 8.____
9. An understanding between him and I was finally reached. 9.____
10. It was at the supervisor's request that the clerk agreed to postpone his vacation. 10.____
11. We do not believe that it is necessary for both he and the clerk to attend the conference. 11.____
12. All employees, who display perseverance, will be given adequate recognition. 12.____
13. He regrets that some of us employees are dissatisfied with our new assignments. 13.____

14. "Do you think that the raise was merited," asked the supervisor? 14._____

15. The new manual of procedure is a valuable supplament to our rules and regulation. 15._____

16. The typist admitted that she had attempted to pursuade the other employees to assist her in her work. 16._____

17. The supervisor asked that all amendments to the regulations be handled by you and I. 17._____

18. They told both he and I that the prisoner had escaped. 18._____

19. Any superior officer, who, disregards the just complaints of his subordinates, is remiss in the performance of his duty. 19._____

20. Only those members of the national organization who resided in the Middle west attended the conference in Chicago. 20._____

21. We told him to give the investigation assignment to whoever was available. 21._____

22. Please do not disappoint and embarass us by not appearing in court. 22._____

23. Despite the efforts of the Supervising mechanic, the elevator could not be started. 23._____

24. The U.S. Weather Bureau, weather record for the accident date was checked. 24._____

KEY (CORRECT ANSWERS)

1.	D		11.	A
2.	A		12.	B
3.	B		13.	D
4.	D		14.	B
5.	D		15.	C
6.	D		16.	C
7.	C		17.	A
8.	A		18.	A
9.	A		19.	B
10.	D		20.	C

21. D
22. C
23. C
24. B

TEST 2

DIRECTIONS: Each question consists of a sentence. Some of the sentences contain errors in English grammar or usage, punctuation, spelling, or capitalization. A sentence does not contain an error simply because it could be written in a different manner. Choose answer:
- A. If the sentence contains an error in English grammar or usage.
- B. if the sentence contains an error in punctuation.
- C. If the sentence contains an error in spelling or capitalization
- D. If the sentence does not contain any errors.

1. The severity of the sentence prescribed by contemporary statutes—including both the former and the revised New York Penal Laws—do not depend on what crime was intended by the offender.

2. It is generally recognized that two defects in the early law of attempt played a part in the birth of burglary: (1) immunity from prosecution for conduct short of the last act before completion of the crime, and (2) the relatively minor penalty imposed for an attempt (it being a common law misdemeanor) vis-à-vis the completed offense.

3. The first sentence of the statute is applicable to employees who enter their place of employment, invited guests, and all other persons who have an express or implied license or privilege to enter the premises.

4. Contemporary criminal codes in the United States generally divide burglary into various degrees, differentiating the categories according to place, time and other attendent circumstances.

5. The assignment was completed in record time but the payroll for it has not yet been prepaid.

6. The operator, on the other hand, is willing to learn me how to use the mimeograph.

7. She is the prettiest of the three sisters.

8. She doesn't know; if the mail has arrived.

9. The doorknob of the office door is broke.

10. Although the department's supply of scratch pads and stationery have diminished considerably, the allotment for our division has not been reduced.

11. You have not told us whom you wish to designate as your secretary.

12. Upon reading the minutes of the last meeting, the new proposal was taken up for consideration.

13. Before beginning the discussion, we locked the door as a precautionery measure.

14. The supervisor remarked, "Only those clerks, who perform routine work, are permitted to take a rest period."

15. Not only will this duplicating machine make accurate copies, but it will also produce a quantity of work equal to fifteen transcribing typists.

16. "Mr. Jones," said the supervisor, "we regret our inability to grant you an extention of your leave of absence."

17. Although the employees find the work monotonous and fatigueing, they rarely complain.

18. We completed the tabulation of the receipts on time despite the fact that Miss Smith our fastest operator was absent for over a week.

19. The reaction of the employees who attended the meeting, as well as the reaction of those who did not attend, indicates clearly that the schedule is satisfactory to everyone concerned.

20. Of the two employees, the one in our office is the most efficient.

21. No one can apply or even understand, the new rules and regulations.

22. A large amount of supplies were stored in the empty office.

23. If an employee is occassionally asked to work overtime, he should do so willingly.

24. It is true that the new procedures are difficult to use but, we are certain that you will learn them quickly.

25. The office manager said that he did not know who would be given a large allotment under the new plan.

KEY (CORRECT ANSWERS)

1.	A	11.	D
2.	D	12.	A
3.	D	13.	C
4.	C	14.	B
5.	C	15.	A
6.	A	16.	C
7.	D	17.	C
8.	B	18.	B
9.	A	19.	D
10.	A	20.	A

21. B
22. A
23. C
24. B
25. D

TEST 3

DIRECTIONS: Each of the following sentences may be classified MOST appropriately under one of the following categories:
   A. Faulty because of incorrect grammar
   B. Faulty because of incorrect punctuation
   C. Faulty because of incorrect capitalization
   D. Correct

Examine each sentence carefully. Then, in the space at the right, print the capital letter preceding the option which is the BEST of the four suggested above. All incorrect sentence contain but one type of error. Consider a sentence correct if it contains none of the types of errors mentioned, even though there may be other correct ways of expressing the same thought.

1. The desk, as well as the chairs, were moved out of the office. 1._____

2. The clerk whose production was greatest for the month won a day's vacation as first prize. 2._____

3. Upon entering the room, the employees were found hard at work at their desks. 3._____

4. John Smith our new employee always arrives at work on time. 4._____

5. Punish whoever is guilty of stealing the money. 5._____

6. Intelligent and persistent effort lead to success no matter what the job may be. 6._____

7. The secretary asked, "can you call again at three o'clock?" 7._____

8. He told us, that if the report was not accepted at the next meeting, it would have to be rewritten. 8._____

9. He would not have sent the letter if he had known that it would cause so much excitement. 9._____

10. We all looked forward to him coming to visit us. 10._____

11. If you find that you are unable to complete the assignment please notify me as soon as possible. 11._____

12. Every girl in the office went home on time but me; there was still some work for me to finish. 12._____

13. He wanted to know who the letter was addressed to, Mr. Brown or Mr. Smith. 13._____

14. "Mr. Jones, he said, please answer this letter as soon as possible." 14._____

15. The new clerk had an unusual accent inasmuch as he was born and educated in the south.   15.____

16. Although he is younger than her, he earns a higher salary.   16.____

17. Neither of the two administrators are going to attend the conference being held in Washington, D.C.   17.____

18. Since Miss Smith and Miss Jones have more experience than us, they have been given more responsible duties.   18.____

19. Mr. Shaw the supervisor of the stock room maintains an inventory of stationery and office supplies.   19.____

20. Inasmuch as this matter affects both you and I, we should take joint action.   20.____

21. Who do you think will be able to perform this highly technical work?   21.____

22. Of the two employees, John is considered the most competent.   22.____

23. He is not coming home on tuesday; we expect him next week.   23.____

24. Stenographers, as well as typists must be able to type rapidly and accurately.   24.____

25. Having been placed in the safe we were sure that the money would not be stolen.   25.____

KEY (CORRECT ANSWERS)

1.	A		11.	B
2.	D		12.	D
3.	A		13.	A
4.	B		14.	B
5.	D		15.	C
6.	A		16.	A
7.	C		17.	A
8.	B		18.	A
9.	D		19.	B
10.	A		20.	A

21. D
22. A
23. C
24. B
25. A

TEST 4

DIRECTIONS: Each of the following sentences consist of four sentences lettered A, B, C, and D. One of the sentences in each group contains an error in grammar or punctuation. Indicate the INCORRECT sentence in each group. *PRINT THE LETTER OF THE CORRECT ANSWER IN THE SPACE AT THE RIGHT.*

1. A. Give the message to whoever is on duty.
   B. The teacher who's pupil won first prize presented the award.
   C. Between you and me, I don't expect the program to succeed.
   D. His running to catch the bus caused the accident.

2. A. The process, which was patented only last year is already obsolete.
   B. His interest in science (which continues to the present) led him to convert his basement into a laboratory.
   C. He described the book as "verbose, repetitious, and bombastic".
   D. Our new director will need to possess three qualities: vision, patience, and fortitude.

3. A. The length of ladder trucks varies considerably.
   B. The probationary fireman reported to the officer to who he was assigned.
   C. The lecturer emphasized the need for we firemen to be punctual.
   D. Neither the officers nor the members of the company knew about the new procedure.

4. A. Ham and eggs is the specialty of the house.
   B. He is one of the students who are on probation.
   C. Do you think that either one of us have a chance to be nominated for president of the class?
   D. I assume that either he was to be in charge or you were.

5. A. Its a long road that has no turn.
   B. To run is more tiring than to walk.
   C. We have been assigned three new reports: namely, the statistical summary, the narrative summary, and the budgetary summary.
   D. Had the first payment been made in January, the second would be due in April.

6. A. Each employer has his own responsibilities.
   B. If a person speaks correctly, they make a good impression.
   C. Every one of the operators has had her vacation.
   D. Has anybody filed his report?

7. A. The manager, with all his salesmen, was obliged to go.
   B. Who besides them is to sign the agreement?
   C. One report without the others is incomplete.
   D. Several clerks, as well as the proprietor, was injured.

2 (#4)

8. A. A suspension of these activities is expected.
    B. The machine is economical because first cost and upkeep are low.
    C. A knowledge of stenography and filing are required for this position.
    D. The condition in which the goods were received shows that the packing was not done properly.

    8._____

9. A. There seems to be a great many reasons for disagreement.
    B. It does not seem possible that they could have failed.
    C. Have there always been too few applicants for these positions?
    D. There is no excuse for these errors.

    9._____

10. A. We shall be pleased to answer your question.
    B. Shall we plan the meeting for Saturday?
    C. I will call you promptly at seven.
    D. Can I borrow your book after you have read it?

    10._____

11. A. You are as capable as I.
    B. Everyone is willing to sign but him and me.
    C. As for he and his assistant, I cannot praise them too highly.
    D. Between you and me, I think he will be dismissed.

    11._____

12. A. Our competitors bid above us last week.
    B. The survey which was began last year has not yet been completed.
    C. The operators had shown that they understood their instructions.
    D. We have never ridden over worse roads.

    12._____

13. A. Who did they say was responsible?
    B. Whom did you suspect?
    C. Who do you suppose it was?
    D. Whom do you mean?

    13._____

14. A. Of the two propositions, this is the worse.
    B. Which report do you consider the best—the one in January or the one in July?
    C. I believe this is the most practicable of the many plans submitted.
    D. He is the youngest employee in the organization.

    14._____

15. A. The firm had but three orders last week.
    B. That doesn't really seem possible.
    C. After twenty years scarcely none of the old business remains.
    D. Has he done nothing about it?

    15._____

KEY (CORRECT ANSWERS)

1.	B	6.	B	11.	C
2.	A	7.	D	12.	B
3.	C	8.	C	13.	A
4.	C	9.	A	14.	B
5.	A	10.	D	15.	C

PREPARING WRITTEN MATERIAL

PARAGRAPH REARRANGEMENT
COMMENTARY

The sentences that follow are in scrambled order. You are to rearrange them in proper order and indicate the letter choice containing the correct answer at the space at the right.

Each group of sentences in this section is actually a paragraph presented in scrambled order. Each sentence in the group has a place in that paragraph; no sentence is to be left out. You are to read each group of sentences and decide upon the best order in which to put the sentences so as to form a well-organized paragraph.

The questions in this section measure the ability to solve a problem when all the facts relevant to its solution are not given.

More specifically, certain positions of responsibility and authority require the employee to discover connection between events sometimes, apparently, unrelated. In order to do this, the employee will find it necessary to correctly infer that unspecified events have probably occurred or are likely to occur. This ability becomes especially important when action must be taken on incomplete information.

Accordingly, these questions require competitors to choose among several suggested alternatives, each of which presents a different sequential arrangement of the events. Competitors must choose the MOST logical of the suggested sequences.

In order to do so, they may be required to draw on general knowledge to infer missing concepts or events that are essential to sequencing the given events. Competitors should be careful to infer only what is essential to the sequence. The plausibility of the wrong alternatives will always require the inclusion of unlikely events or of additional chains of events which are NOT essential to sequencing the given events.

It's very important to remember that you are looking for the best of the four possible choices, and that the best choice of all may not even be one of the answers you're given to choose from.

There is no one right way to solve these problems. Many people have found it helpful to first write out the order of the sentences, as they would have arranged them, on their scrap paper before looking at the possible answers. If their optimum answer is there, this can save them some time. If it isn't, this method can still give insight into solving the problem. Others find it most helpful to just go through each of the possible choices, contrasting each as they go along. You should use whatever method feels comfortable and works for you.

While most of these types of questions are not that difficult, we've added a higher percentage of the difficult type, just to give you more practice. Usually there are only one or two questions on this section that contain such subtle distinctions that you're unable to answer confidently. And you then may find yourself stuck deciding between two possible choices, neither of which you're sure about.

EXAMINATION SECTION

TEST 1

DIRECTIONS: Each question consists of several sentences which can be arranged in a logical sequence. For each question, select the choice which places the numbered sentences in the MOST logical sequence. *PRINT THE LETTER OF THE CORRECT ANSWER IN THE SPACE AT THE RIGHT.*

1. I. A body was found in the woods.
   II. A man proclaimed innocence.
   III. The owner of a gun was located.
   IV. A gun was traced.
   V. The owner of a gun was questioned.
   The CORRECT answer is:
   A. IV, III, V, II, I
   B. II, I, IV, III, V
   C. I, IV, III, V, II
   D. I, III, V, II, IV
   E. I, II, IV, III, V

   1.____

2. I. A man is in a hunting accident.
   II. A man fell down a flight of steps.
   III. A man lost his vision in one eye.
   IV. A man broke his leg.
   V. A man had to walk with a cane.
   The CORRECT answer is:
   A. II, IV, V, I, III
   B. IV, V, I, III, II
   C. III, I, IV, V, II
   D. I, III, V, II, IV
   E. I, III, II, IV, V

   2.____

3. I. A man is offered a new job.
   II. A woman is offered a new job.
   III. A man works as a waiter.
   IV. A woman works as a waitress.
   V. A woman gives notice.
   The CORRECT answer is:
   A. IV, II, V, III, I
   B. IV, II, V, I, III
   C. II, IV, V, III, I
   D. III, I, IV, II, V
   E. IV, III, II, V, I

   3.____

4. I. A train let the station late.
   II. A man was late for work.
   III. A man lost his job.
   IV. Many people complained because the train was late.
   V. There was a traffic jam.
   The CORRECT answer is:
   A. V, II, I, IV, III
   B. V, I, IV, II, III
   C. V, I, II, IV, III
   D. I, V, IV, II, III
   E. II, I, IV, V, III

   4.____

105

5. I. The burden of proof as to each issue is determined before trial and remains upon the same party throughout the trial.
    II. The jury is at liberty to believe one witness' testimony as against a number of contradictory witnesses.
    III. In a civil case, the party bearing the burden of proof is required to prove his contention by a fair preponderance of the evidence.
    IV. However, it must be noted that a fair preponderance of evidence does not necessarily mean a greater number of witnesses.
    V. The burden of proof is the burden which rests upon one of the parties to an action to persuade the trier of the facts, generally the jury, that a proposition he asserts is true.
    VI. If the evidence is equally balanced, or if it leaves the jury in such doubt as to be unable to decide the controversy either way, judgment must be given against the party upon whom the burden of proof rests.
    The CORRECT answer is:
    A. III. II, V, IV, I, VI B. I, II, VI, V, III, IV C. III, IV, V, I, II, VI
    D. V, I, III, VI, IV, II E. I, V, III, VI, IV, II

6. I. If a parent is without assets and is unemployed, he cannot be convicted of the crime of non-support of a child.
    II. The term *sufficient ability* has been held to mean sufficient financial ability.
    III. It does not matter if his unemployment is by choice or unavoidable circumstances.
    IV. If he fails to take any steps at all, he may be liable to prosecution for endangering the welfare of a child.
    V. Under the penal law, a parent is responsible for the support of his minor child only if the parent is of *sufficient ability*.
    VI. An indigent parent may meet his obligation by borrowing money or by seeking aid under the provisions of the Social Welfare Law.
    The CORRECT answer is:
    A. VI, I, V, III, II, IV B. I, III, V, II, IV, VI C. V, II, I, III, VI, IV
    D. I, VI, IV, V, II, III E. II, V, I, III, VI, IV

7. I. Consider, for example, the case of a rabble rouser who urges a group of twenty people to go out and break the windows of a nearby factory.
    II. Therefore, the law fills the indicated gap with the crime of *inciting to riot*.
    III. A person is considered guilty of inciting to riot when he urges ten or more persons to engage in tumultuous and violent conduct of a kind likely to create public alarm.
    IV. However, if he has not obtained the cooperation of at least four people, he cannot be charged with unlawful assembly.
    V. The charge of inciting to riot was added to the law to cover types of conduct which cannot be classified as either the crime of *riot* or the crime of *unlawful assembly*.
    VI. If he acquires the acquiescence of at least four of them, he is guilty of unlawful assembly even if the project does not materialize.
    The CORRECT answer is:
    A. III, V, I, VI, IV, II B. V, I, IV, VI, II, III C. III, IV, I, V, II, VI
    D. V, I, IV, VI, III, II E. V, III, I, VI, IV, II

8. I. If, however, the rebuttal evidence presents an issue of credibility, it is for the jury to determine whether the presumption has, in fact, been destroyed.
    II. Once sufficient evidence to the contrary is introduced, the presumption disappears from the trial.
    III. The effect of a presumption is to place the burden upon the adversary to come forward with evidence to rebut the presumption.
    IV. When a presumption is overcome and ceases to exist in the case, the fact or facts which gave rise to the presumption still remain.
    V. Whether a presumption has been overcome is ordinarily a question for the court.
    VI. Such information may furnish a basis for a logical inference.
    The CORRECT answer is:
    A. IV, VI, II, V, I, III
    B. III, II, V, I, IV, VI
    C. V, III, VI, IV, II, I
    D. V, IV, I, II, VI, III
    E. II, III, V, I, IV, VI

9. I. An executive may answer a letter by writing his reply on the face of the letter itself instead of having a return letter typed.
    II. This procedure is efficient because it saves the executive's time, the typist's time, and saves office file space.
    III. Copying machines are used in small offices as well as large offices to save time and money in making brief replies to business letters.
    IV. A copy is made on a copying machine to go into the company files, while the original is mailed back to the sender.
    The CORRECT answer is:
    A. I, II, IV, III
    B. I, IV, II, III
    C. III, I, IV, II
    D. III, IV, II, I

10. I. Most organizations favor one of the types but always include the others to a lesser degree.
    II. However, we can detect a definite trend toward greater use of symbolic control.
    III. We suggest that our local police agencies are today primarily utilizing material control.
    IV. Control can be classified into three types: physical, material, and symbolic.
    The CORRECT answer is:
    A. IV, II, III, I
    B. II, I, IV, III
    C. III, IV, II, I
    D. IV, I, III, II

11. I. Project residents had first claim to this use, followed by surrounding neighborhood children.
    II. By contrast, recreation space within the project's interior was found to be used more often by both groups.
    III. Studies of the use of project grounds in many cities showed grounds left open for public use were neglected and unused, both by residents and by members of the surrounding community.
    IV. Project residents had clearly laid claim to the play spaces, setting up and enforcing unwritten rules for use.
    V. Each group, by experience, found their activities easily disrupted by other groups, and their claim to the use of space for recreation difficult to enforce.

The CORRECT answer is:
A. IV, V, I, II, III
B. V, II, IV, III, I
C. I, IV, III, II, V
D. III, V, II, IV, I

12. I. They do not consider the problems correctable within the existing subsidy formula and social policy of accepting all eligible applicants regardless of social behavior.
    II. A recent survey, however, indicated that tenants believe these problems correctable by local housing authorities and management within the existing financial formula.
    III. Many of the problems and complaints concerning public housing management and design have created resentment between the tenant and the landlord.
    IV. This same survey indicated that administrators and managers do not agree with the tenants.
    The CORRECT answer is:
    A. II, I, III, IV   B. I, III, IV, II   C. III, II, IV, I   D. IV, II, I, III

13. I. In single-family residences, there is usually enough distance between tenants to prevent occupants from annoying one another.
    II. For example, a certain small percentage of tenant families has one or more members addicted to alcohol.
    III. While managers believe in the right of individuals to live as they choose, the manager becomes concerned when the pattern of living jeopardizes others' rights.
    IV. Still others turn night into day, staging lusty entertainments which carry on into the hours when most tenants are trying to sleep.
    V. In apartment buildings, however, tenants live so closely together that any misbehavior can result in unpleasant living conditions.
    VI. Other families engage in violent argument.
    The CORRECT answer is:
    A. III, II, V, IV, VI, I
    B. I, V, II, VI, IV, III
    C. II, V, IV, I, III, VI
    D. IV, II, V, VI, III, I

14. I. Congress made the commitment explicit in the Housing Act of 194, establishing as a national goal the realization of a *decent home and suitable environment for every American family*.
    II. The result has been that the goal of decent home and suitable environment is still as far distant as ever for the disadvantaged urban family.
    III. In spite of this action by Congress, federal housing programs have continued to be fragmented and grossly underfunded.
    IV. The passage of the National Housing Act signaled a few federal commitment to provide housing for the nation's citizens.
    The CORRECT answer is:
    A. I, IV, III, II   B. IV, I, III, II   C. IV, I, II, III   D. II, IV, I, III

15.
I. The greater expense does not necessarily involve *exploitation*, but it is often perceived as exploitative and unfair by those who are aware of the price differences involved, but unaware of operating costs.
II. Ghetto residents believe they are *exploited* by local merchants, and evidence substantiates some of these beliefs.
III. However, stores in low-income areas were more likely to be small independents, which could not achieve the economies available to supermarket chains and were, therefore, more likely to charge higher prices, and the customers were more likely to buy smaller-sized packages which are more expensive per unit of measure.
IV. A study conducted in one city showed that distinctly higher prices were charged for goods sold in ghetto stores in other areas.
The CORRECT answer is:
A. IV, II, I, III   B. IV, I, III, II   C. II, IV, III, I   D. II, III, IV, I

15.____

KEY (CORRECT ANSWERS)

1. C   6. C   11. D
2. E   7. A   12. C
3. B   8. B   13. B
4. B   9. C   14. B
5. D   10. D   15. C

PHILOSOPHY, PRINCIPLES, PRACTICES, AND TECHNICS OF SUPERVISION, ADMINISTRATION, MANAGEMENT, AND ORGANIZATION

TABLE OF CONTENTS

	Page
MEANING OF SUPERVISION	1
THE OLD AND THE NEW SUPERVISION	1
THE EIGHT (8) BASIC PRINCIPLES OF THE NEW SUPERVISION	1
I. Principle of Responsibility	1
II. Principle of Authority	2
III. Principle of Self-Growth	2
IV. Principle of Individual Worth	2
V. Principle of Creative Leadership	2
VI. Principle of Success and Failure	2
VII. Principle of Science	3
VIII. Principle of Cooperation	3
WHAT IS ADMINISTRATION?	3
I. Practices Commonly Classed as "Supervisory"	3
II. Practices Commonly Classed as "Administrative"	3
III. Practices Commonly Classed as Both "Supervisory" and "Administrative"	4
RESPONSIBILITIES OF THE SUPERVISOR	4
COMPETENCIES OF THE SUPERVISOR	4
THE PROFESSIONAL SUPERVISOR-EMPLOYEE RELATIONSHIP	4
MINI-TEXT IN SUPERVISION, ADMINISTRATION, MANAGEMENT, AND ORGANIZATION	5
I. Brief Highlights	5
A. Levels of Management	6
B. What the Supervisor Must Learn	6
C. A Definition of Supervision	6
D. Elements of the Team Concept	6
E. Principles of Organization	6
F. The Four Important Parts of Every Job	7
G. Principles of Delegation	7
H. Principles of Effective Communications	7
I. Principles of Work Improvement	7
J. Areas of Job Improvement	7
K. Seven Key Points in Making Improvements	8

	L.	Corrective Techniques for Job Improvement	8
	M.	A Planning Checklist	8
	N.	Five Characteristics of Good Directions	9
	O.	Types of Directions	9
	P.	Controls	9
	Q.	Orienting the New Employee	9
	R.	Checklist for Orienting New Employees	9
	S.	Principles of Learning	10
	T.	Causes of Poor Performance	10
	U.	Four Major Steps in On-the-Job Instructions	10
	V.	Employees Want Five Things	10
	W.	Some Don'ts in Regard to Praise	11
	X.	How to Gain Your Workers' Confidence	11
	Y.	Sources of Employee Problems	11
	Z.	The Supervisor's Key to Discipline	11
	AA.	Five Important Processes of Management	12
	BB.	When the Supervisor Fails to Plan	12
	CC.	Fourteen General Principles of Management	12
	DD.	Change	12
II.	Brief Topical Summaries		13
	A.	Who/What is the Supervisor?	13
	B.	The Sociology of Work	13
	C.	Principles and Practices of Supervision	14
	D.	Dynamic Leadership	14
	E.	Processes for Solving Problems	15
	F.	Training for Results	15
	G.	Health, Safety, and Accident Prevention	16
	H.	Equal Employment Opportunity	16
	I.	Improving Communications	16
	J.	Self-Development	17
	K.	Teaching and Training	17
		1. The Teaching Process	17
		a. Preparation	17
		b. Presentation	18
		c. Summary	18
		d. Application	18
		e. Evaluation	18
		2. Teaching Methods	18
		a. Lecture	18
		b. Discussion	18
		c. Demonstration	19
		d. Performance	19
		e. Which Method to Use	19

PHILOSOPHY, PRINCIPLES, PRACTICES, AND TECHNICS
OF
SUPERVISION, ADMINISTRATION, MANAGEMENT, AND ORGANIZATION

MEANING OF SUPERVISION

The extension of the democratic philosophy has been accompanied by an extension in the scope of supervision. Modern leaders and supervisors no longer think of supervision in the narrow sense of being confined chiefly to visiting employees, supplying materials, or rating the staff. They regard supervision as being intimately related to all the concerned agencies of society, they speak of the supervisor's function in terms of "growth," rather than the "improvement" of employees.

This modern concept of supervision may be defined as follows: Supervision is leadership and the development of leadership within groups which are cooperatively engaged in inspection, research, training, guidance, and evaluation.

THE OLD AND THE NEW SUPERVISION

TRADITIONAL
1. Inspection
2. Focused on the employee
3. Visitation
4. Random and haphazard
5. Imposed and authoritarian
6. One person usually

MODERN
1. Study and analysis
2. Focused on aims, materials, methods, supervisors, employees, environment
3. Demonstrations, intervisitation, workshops, directed reading, bulletins, etc.
4. Definitely organized and planned (scientific)
5. Cooperative and democratic
6. Many persons involved (creative)

THE EIGHT (8) BASIC PRINCIPLES OF THE NEW SUPERVISION

I. Principle of Responsibility
   Authority to act and responsibility for acting must be joined.
   A. If you give responsibility, give authority.
   B. Define employee duties clearly.
   C. Protect employees from criticism by others.
   D. Recognize the rights as well as obligations of employees.
   E. Achieve the aims of a democratic society insofar as it is possible within the area of your work.
   F. Establish a situation favorable to training and learning.
   G. Accept ultimate responsibility for everything done in your section, unit, office, division, department.
   H. Good administration and good supervision are inseparable.

II. Principle of Authority
The success of the supervisor is measured by the extent to which the power of authority is not used.
   A. Exercise simplicity and informality in supervision
   B. Use the simplest machinery of supervision
   C. If it is good for the organization as a whole, it is probably justified.
   D. Seldom be arbitrary or authoritative.
   E. Do not base your work on the power of position or of personality.
   F. Permit and encourage the free expression of opinions.

III. Principle of Self-Growth
The success of the supervisor is measured by the extent to which, and the speed with which, he is no longer needed.
   A. Base criticism on principles, not on specifics.
   B. Point out higher activities to employees.
   C. Train for self-thinking by employees to meet new situations.
   D. Stimulate initiative, self-reliance, and individual responsibility
   E. Concentrate on stimulating the growth of employees rather than on removing defects.

IV. Principle of Individual Worth
Respect for the individual is a paramount consideration in supervision.
   A. Be human and sympathetic in dealing with employees.
   B. Don't nag about things to be done.
   C. Recognize the individual differences among employees and seek opportunities to permit best expression of each personality.

V. Principle of Creative Leadership
The best supervision is that which is not apparent to the employee.
   A. Stimulate, don't drive employees to creative action.
   B. Emphasize doing good things.
   C. Encourage employees to do what they do best.
   D. Do not be too greatly concerned with details of subject or method.
   E. Do not be concerned exclusively with immediate problems and activities.
   F. Reveal higher activities and make them both desired and maximally possible.
   G. Determine procedures in the light of each situation but see that these are derived from a sound basic philosophy.
   H. Aid, inspire, and lead so as to liberate the creative spirit latent in all good employees.

VI. Principle of Success and Failure
There are no unsuccessful employees, only unsuccessful supervisors who have failed to give proper leadership.
   A. Adapt suggestions to the capacities, attitudes, and prejudices of employees.
   B. Be gradual, be progressive, be persistent.
   C. Help the employee find the general principle; have the employee apply his own problem to the general principle.
   D. Give adequate appreciation for good work and honest effort.
   E. Anticipate employee difficulties and help to prevent them.
   F. Encourage employees to do the desirable things they will do anyway.
   G. Judge your supervision by the results it secures.

VII. Principle of Science
Successful supervision is scientific, objective, and experimental. It is based on facts, not on prejudices.
   A. Be cumulative in results.
   B. Never divorce your suggestions from the goals of training.
   C. Don't be impatient of results.
   D. Keep all matters on a professional, not a personal, level.
   E. Do not be concerned exclusively with immediate problems and activities.
   F. Use objective means of determining achievement and rating where possible.

VIII. Principle of Cooperation
Supervision is a cooperative enterprise between supervisor and employee.
   A. Begin with conditions as they are.
   B. Ask opinions of all involved when formulating policies.
   C. Organization is as good as its weakest link.
   D. Let employees help to determine policies and department programs.
   E. Be approachable and accessible—physically and mentally.
   F. Develop pleasant social relationships.

WHAT IS ADMINISTRATION

Administration is concerned with providing the environment, the material facilities, and the operational procedures that will promote the maximum growth and development of supervisors and employees. (Organization is an aspect and a concomitant of administration.)

There is no sharp line of demarcation between supervision and administration; these functions are intimately interrelated and, often, overlapping. They are complementary activities.

I. Practices Commonly Classed as "Supervisory"
   A. Conducting employees' conferences
   B. Visiting sections, units, offices, divisions, departments
   C. Arranging for demonstrations
   D. Examining plans
   E. Suggesting professional reading
   F. Interpreting bulletins
   G. Recommending in-service training courses
   H. Encouraging experimentation
   I. Appraising employee morale
   J. Providing for intervisitation

II. Practices Commonly Classified as "Administrative"
   A. Management of the office
   B. Arrangement of schedules for extra duties
   C. Assignment of rooms or areas
   D. Distribution of supplies
   E. Keeping records and reports
   F. Care of audio-visual materials
   G. Keeping inventory records
   H. Checking record cards and books

I. Programming special activities
  J. Checking on the attendance and punctuality of employees

III. Practices Commonly Classified as Both "Supervisory" and "Administrative"
  A. Program construction
  B. Testing or evaluating outcomes
  C. Personnel accounting
  D. Ordering instructional materials

RESPONSIBILITIES OF THE SUPERVISOR

A person employed in a supervisory capacity must constantly be able to improve his own efficiency and ability. He represent the employer to the employees and only continuous self-examination can make him a capable supervisor.

Leadership and training are the supervisor's responsibility. An efficient working unit is one in which the employees work with the supervisor. It is his job to bring out the best in his employees. He must always be relaxed, courteous, and calm in his association with his employees. Their feelings are important, and a harsh attitude does not develop the most efficient employees.

COMPETENCES OF THE SUPERVISOR

  I. Complete knowledge of the duties and responsibilities of his position.
  II. To be able to organize a job, plan ahead, and carry through.
  III. To have self-confidence and initiative.
  IV. To be able to handle the unexpected situation and make quick decisions.
  V. To be able to properly train subordinates in the positions they are best suited for.
  VI. To be able to keep good human relations among his subordinates.
  VII. To be able to keep good human relations between his subordinates and himself and to earn their respect and trust.

THE PROFESSIONAL SUPERVISOR-EMPLOYEE RELATIONSHIP

There are two kinds of efficiency: one kind is only apparent and is produced in organizations through the exercise of mere discipline; this is but a simulation of the second, or true, efficiency which springs from spontaneous cooperation. If you are a manager, no matter how great or small your responsibility, it is your job, in the final analysis, to create and develop this involuntary cooperation among the people whom you supervise. For, no matter how powerful a combination of money, machines, and materials a company may have, this is a dead and sterile thing without a team of willing, thinking, and articulate people to guide it.

The following 21 points are presented as indicative of the exemplary basic relationship that should exist between supervisor and employee:

1. Each person wants to be liked and respected by his fellow employee and wants to be treated with consideration and respect by his superior.
2. The most competent employee will make an error. However, in a unit where good relations exist between the supervisor and his employees, tenseness and fear do not exist. Thus, errors are not hidden or covered up, and the efficiency of a unit is not impaired.

3. Subordinates resent rules, regulations, or orders that are unreasonable or unexplained.
4. Subordinates are quick to resent unfairness, harshness, injustices, and favoritism.
5. An employee will accept responsibility if he knows that he will be complimented for a job well done, and not too harshly chastised for failure; that his supervisor will check the cause of the failure, and, if it was the supervisor's fault, he will assume the blame therefore. If it was the employee's fault, his supervisor will explain the correct method or means of handling the responsibility.
6. An employee wants to receive credit for a suggestion he has made, that is used. If a suggestion cannot be used, the employee is entitled to an explanation. The supervisor should not say "no" and close the subject.
7. Fear and worry slow up a worker's ability. Poor working environment can impair his physical and mental health. A good supervisor avoids forceful methods, threats, and arguments to get a job done.
8. A forceful supervisor is able to train his employees individually and as a team, and is able to motivate them in the proper channels.
9. A mature supervisor is able to properly evaluate his subordinates and to keep them happy and satisfied.
10. A sensitive supervisor will never patronize his subordinates.
11. A worthy supervisor will respect his employees' confidences.
12. Definite and clear-cut responsibilities should be assigned to each executive.
13. Responsibility should always be coupled with corresponding authority.
14. No change should be made in the scope or responsibilities of a position without a definite understanding to that effect on the part of all persons concerned.
15. No executive or employee, occupying a single position in the organization, should be subject to definite orders from more than one source.
16. Orders should never be given to subordinates over the head of a responsible executive. Rather than do this, the officer in question should be supplanted.
17. Criticisms of subordinates should, whoever possible, be made privately, and in no case should a subordinate be criticized in the presence of executives or employees of equal or lower rank.
18. No dispute or difference between executives or employees as to authority or responsibilities should be considered too trivial for prompt and careful adjudication.
19. Promotions, wage changes, and disciplinary action should always be approved by the executive immediately superior to the one directly responsible.
20. No executive or employee should ever be required, or expected, to be at the same time an assistant to, and critic of, another.
21. Any executive whose work is subject to regular inspection should, wherever practicable, be given the assistance and facilities necessary to enable him to maintain an independent check of the quality of his work.

MINI-TEXT IN SUPERVISION, ADMINISTRATION, MANAGEMENT, AND ORGANIZATION

I. Brief Highlights

Listed concisely and sequentially are major headings and important data in the field for quick recall and review.

A. Levels of Management
Any organization of some size has several levels of management. In terms of a ladder, the levels are:

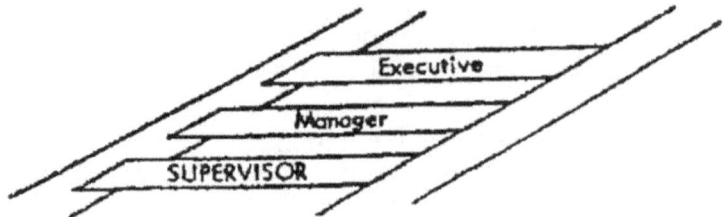

The first level is very important because it is the beginning point of management leadership.

B. What the Supervisor Must Learn
A supervisor must learn to:
1. Deal with people and their differences
2. Get the job done through people
3. Recognize the problems when they exist
4. Overcome obstacles to good performance
5. Evaluate the performance of people
6. Check his own performance in terms of accomplishment

C. A Definition of Supervisor
The term supervisor means any individual having authority, in the interests of the employer, to hire, transfer, suspend, lay-off, recall, promote, discharge, assign, reward, or discipline other employees or responsibility to direct them, or to adjust their grievances, or effectively to recommend such action, if, in connection with the foregoing, exercise of such authority is not of a merely routine or clerical nature but requires the use of independent judgment.

D. Elements of the Team Concept
What is involved in teamwork? The component parts are:
1. Members
2. A leader
3. Goals
4. Plans
5. Cooperation
6. Spirit

E. Principles of Organization
1. A team member must know what his job is.
2. Be sure that the nature and scope of a job are understood.
3. Authority and responsibility should be carefully spelled out.
4. A supervisor should be permitted to make the maximum number of decisions affecting his employees.
5. Employees should report to only one supervisor.
6. A supervisor should direct only as many employees as he can handle effectively.
7. An organization plan should be flexible.

8. Inspection and performance of work should be separate.
9. Organizational problems should receive immediate attention.
10. Assign work in line with ability and experience.

F. The Four Important Parts of Every Job
1. Inherent in every job is the *accountability* for results.
2. A second set of factors in every job is *responsibilities*.
3. Along with duties and responsibilities one must have the *authority* to act within certain limits without obtaining permission to proceed.
4. No job exists in a vacuum. The supervisor is surrounded by key *relationships*.

G. Principles of Delegation
Where work is delegated for the first time, the supervisor should think in terms of these questions:
1. Who is best qualified to do this?
2. Can an employee improve his abilities by doing this?
3. How long should an employee spend on this?
4. Are there any special problems for which he will need guidance?
5. How broad a delegation can I make?

H. Principles of Effective Communications
1. Determine the media.
2. To whom directed?
3. Identification and source authority.
4. Is communication understood?

I. Principles of Work Improvement
1. Most people usually do only the work which is assigned to them.
2. Workers are likely to fit assigned work into the time available to perform it.
3. A good workload usually stimulates output.
4. People usually do their best work when they know that results will be reviewed or inspected.
5. Employees usually feel that someone else is responsible for conditions of work, workplace layout, job methods, type of tools/equipment, and other such factors.
6. Employees are usually defensive about their job security.
7. Employees have natural resistance to change.
8. Employees can support or destroy a supervisor.
9. A supervisor usually earns the respect of his people through his personal example of diligence and efficiency.

J. Areas of Job Improvement
The areas of job improvement are quite numerous, but the most common ones which a supervisor can identify and utilize are:
1. Departmental layout
2. Flow of work
3. Workplace layout
4. Utilization of manpower
5. Work methods
6. Materials handling

7. Utilization
8. Motion economy

K. Seven Key Points in Making Improvements
1. Select the job to be improved
2. Study how it is being done now
3. Question the present method
4. Determine actions to be taken
5. Chart proposed method
6. Get approval and apply
7. Solicit worker participation

l. Corrective Techniques of Job Improvement
Specific Problems
1. Size of workload
2. Inability to meet schedules
3. Strain and fatigue
4. Improper use of men and skills
5. Waste, poor quality, unsafe conditions
6. Bottleneck conditions that hinder output
7. Poor utilization of equipment and machine
8. Efficiency and productivity of labor

General Improvement
1. Departmental layout
2. Flow of work
3. Work plan layout
4. Utilization of manpower
5. Work methods
6. Materials handling
7. Utilization of equipment
8. Motion economy

Corrective Techniques
1. Study with scale model
2. Flow chart study
3. Motion analysis
4. Comparison of units produced to standard allowance
5. Methods analysis
6. Flow chart and equipment study
7. Down time vs. running time
8. Motion analysis

M. A Planning Checklist
1. Objectives
2. Controls
3. Delegations
4. Communications
5. Resources
6. Manpower

7. Equipment
8. Supplies and materials
9. Utilization of time
10. Safety
11. Money
12. Work
13. Timing of improvements

N. Five Characteristics of Good Directions
In order to get results, directions must be:
1. Possible of accomplishment
2. Agreeable with worker interests
3. Related to mission
4. Planned and complete
5. Unmistakably clear

O. Types of Directions
1. Demands or direct orders
2. Requests
3. Suggestion or implication
4. volunteering

P. Controls
A typical listing of the overall areas in which the supervisor should establish controls might be:
1. Manpower
2. Materials
3. Quality of work
4. Quantity of work
5. Time
6. Space
7. Money
8. Methods

Q. Orienting the New Employee
1. Prepare for him
2. Welcome the new employee
3. Orientation for the job
4. Follow-up

R. Checklist for Orienting New Employees   Yes   No
1. Do you appreciate the feelings of new employees when they first report for work?   ___   ___
2. Are you aware of the fact that the new employee must make a big adjustment to his job?   ___   ___
3. Have you given him good reasons for liking the job and the organization?   ___   ___
4. Have you prepared for his first day on the job?   ___   ___
5. Did you welcome him cordially and make him feel needed?   ___   ___

		Yes	No

6. Did you establish rapport with him so that he feels free to talk and discuss matters with you? ___ ___
7. Did you explain his job to him and his relationship to you? ___ ___
8. Does he know that his work will be evaluated periodically on a basis that is fair and objective? ___ ___
9. Did you introduce him to his fellow workers in such a way that they are likely to accept him? ___ ___
10. Does he know what employee benefits he will receive? ___ ___
11. Does he understand the importance of being on the job and what to do if he must leave his duty station? ___ ___
12. Has he been impressed with the importance of accident prevention and safe practice? ___ ___
13. Does he generally know his way around the department? ___ ___
14. Is he under the guidance of a sponsor who will teach the right way of doing things? ___ ___
15. Do you plan to follow-up so that he will continue to adjust successfully to his job? ___ ___

S. Principles of Learning
 1. Motivation
 2. Demonstration or explanation
 3. Practice

T. Causes of Poor Performance
 1. Improper training for job
 2. Wrong tools
 3. Inadequate directions
 4. Lack of supervisory follow-up
 5. Poor communications
 6. Lack of standards of performance
 7. Wrong work habits
 8. Low morale
 9. Other

U. Four Major Steps in On-The-Job Instruction
 1. Prepare the worker
 2. Present the operation
 3. Tryout performance
 4. Follow-up

V. Employees Want Five Things
 1. Security
 2. Opportunity
 3. Recognition
 4. Inclusion
 5. Expression

W. Some Don'ts in Regard to Praise
 1. Don't praise a person for something he hasn't done.
 2. Don't praise a person unless you can be sincere.
 3. Don't be sparing in praise just because your superior withholds it from you.
 4. Don't let too much time elapse between good performance and recognition of it

X. How to Gain Your Workers' Confidence
 Methods of developing confidence include such things as:
 1. Knowing the interests, habits, hobbies of employees
 2. Admitting your own inadequacies
 3. Sharing and telling of confidence in others
 4. Supporting people when they are in trouble
 5. Delegating matters that can be well handled
 6. Being frank and straightforward about problems and working conditions
 7. Encouraging others to bring their problems to you
 8. Taking action on problems which impede worker progress

Y. Sources of Employee Problems
 On-the-job causes might be such things as:
 1. A feeling that favoritism is exercised in assignments
 2. Assignment of overtime
 3. An undue amount of supervision
 4. Changing methods or systems
 5. Stealing of ideas or trade secrets
 6. Lack of interest in job
 7. Threat of reduction in force
 8. Ignorance or lack of communications
 9. Poor equipment
 10. Lack of knowing how supervisor feels toward employee
 11. Shift assignments

 Off-the-job problems might have to do with:
 1. Health
 2. Finances
 3. Housing
 4. Family

Z. The Supervisor's Key to Discipline
 There are several key points about discipline which the supervisor should keep in mind:
 1. Job discipline is one of the disciplines of life and is directed by the supervisor.
 2. It is more important to correct an employee fault than to fix blame for it.
 3. Employee performance is affected by problems both on the job and off.
 4. Sudden or abrupt changes in behavior can be indications of important employee problems.
 5. Problems should be dealt with as soon as possible after they are identified.
 6. The attitude of the supervisor may have more to do with solving problems than the techniques of problem solving.
 7. Correction of employee behavior should be resorted to only after the supervisor is sure that training or counseling will not be helpful.

8. Be sure to document your disciplinary actions.
9. Make sure that you are disciplining on the basis of facts rather than personal feelings.
10. Take each disciplinary step in order, being careful not to make snap judgments, or decisions based on impatience.

AA. Five Important Processes of Management
1. Planning
2. Organizing
3. Scheduling
4. Controlling
5. Motivating

BB. When the Supervisor Fails to Plan
1. Supervisor creates impression of not knowing his job
2. May lead to excessive overtime
3. Job runs itself—supervisor lacks control
4. Deadlines and appointments missed
5. Parts of the work go undone
6. Work interrupted by emergencies
7. Sets a bad example
8. Uneven workload creates peaks and valleys
9. Too much time on minor details at expense of more important tasks

CC. Fourteen General Principles of Management
1. Division of work
2. Authority and responsibility
3. Discipline
4. Unity of command
5. Unity of direction
6. Subordination of individual interest to general interest
7. Remuneration of personnel
8. Centralization
9. Scalar chain
10. Order
11. Equity
12. Stability of tenure of personnel
13. Initiative
14. Esprit de corps

DD. Change

Bringing about change is perhaps attempted more often, and yet less well understood, than anything else the supervisor does. How do people generally react to change? (People tend to resist change that is imposed upon them by other individuals or circumstances.

Change is characteristic of every situation. It is a part of every real endeavor where the efforts of people are concerned.

13

1. Why do people resist change?
   People may resist change because of:
   a. Fear of the unknown
   b. Implied criticism
   c. Unpleasant experiences in the past
   d. Fear of loss of status
   e. Threat to the ego
   f. Fear of loss of economic stability

2. How can we best overcome the resistance to change?
   In initiating change, take these steps:
   a. Get ready to sell
   b. Identify sources of help
   c. Anticipate objections
   d. Sell benefits
   e. Listen in depth
   f. Follow up

II. Brief Topical Summaries

   A. Who/What is the Supervisor?
      1. The supervisor is often called the "highest level employee and the lowest level manager."
      2. A supervisor is a member of both management and the work group. He acts as a bridge between the two.
      3. Most problems in supervision are in the area of human relations, or people problems.
      4. Employees expect: Respect, opportunity to learn and to advance, and a sense of belonging, and so forth.
      5. Supervisors are responsible for directing people and organizing work. Planning is of paramount importance.
      6. A position description is a set of duties and responsibilities inherent to a given position.
      7. It is important to keep the position description up-to-date and to provide each employee with his own copy.

   B. The Sociology of Work
      1. People are alike in many ways; however, each individual is unique.
      2. The supervisor is challenged in getting to know employee differences. Acquiring skills in evaluating individuals is an asset.
      3. Maintaining meaningful working relationships in the organization is of great importance.
      4. The supervisor has an obligation to help individuals to develop to their fullest potential.
      5. Job rotation on a planned basis helps to build versatility and to maintain interest and enthusiasm in work groups.
      6. Cross training (job rotation) provides backup skills.

7. The supervisor can help reduce tension by maintaining a sense of humor, providing guidance to employees, and by making reasonable and timely decisions. Employees respond favorably to working under reasonably predictable circumstances.
8. Change is characteristic of all managerial behavior. The supervisor must adjust to changes in procedures, new methods, technological changes, and to a number of new and sometimes challenging situations.
9. To overcome the natural tendency for people to resist change, the supervisor should become more skillful in initiating change.

C. Principles and Practices of Supervision
1. Employees should be required to answer to only one superior.
2. A supervisor can effectively direct only a limited number of employees, depending upon the complexity, variety, and proximity of the jobs involved.
3. The organizational chart presents the organization in graphic form. It reflects lines of authority and responsibility as well as interrelationships of units within the organization.
4. Distribution of work can be improved through an analysis using the "Work Distribution Chart."
5. The "Work Distribution Chart" reflects the division of work within a unit in understandable form.
6. When related tasks are given to an employee, he has a better chance of increasing his skills through training.
7. The individual who is given the responsibility for tasks must also be given the appropriate authority to insure adequate results.
8. The supervisor should delegate repetitive, routine work. Preparation of recurring reports, maintaining leave and attendance records are some examples.
9. Good discipline is essential to good task performance. Discipline is reflected in the actions of employees on the job in the absence of supervision.
10. Disciplinary action may have to be taken when the positive aspects of discipline have failed. Reprimand, warning, and suspension are examples of disciplinary action.
11. If a situation calls for a reprimand, be sure it is deserved and remember it is to be done in private.

D. Dynamic Leadership
1. A style is a personal method or manner of exerting influence.
2. Authoritarian leaders often see themselves as the source of power and authority.
3. The democratic leader often perceives the group as the source of authority and power.
4. Supervisors tend to do better when using the pattern of leadership that is most natural for them.
5. Social scientists suggest that the effective supervisor use the leadership style that best fits the problem or circumstances involved.
6. All four styles—telling, selling, consulting, joining—have their place. Using one does not preclude using the other at another time.

7. The theory X point of view assumes that the average person dislikes work, will avoid it whenever possible, and must be coerced to achieve organizational objectives.
8. The theory Y point of view assumes that the average person considers work to be a natural as play, and, when the individual is committed, he requires little supervision or direction to accomplish desired objectives.
9. The leader's basic assumptions concerning human behavior and human nature affect his actions, decisions, and other managerial practices.
10. Dissatisfaction among employees is often present, but difficult to isolate. The supervisor should seek to weaken dissatisfaction by keeping promises, being sincere and considerate, keeping employees informed, and so forth.
11. Constructive suggestions should be encouraged during the natural progress of the work.

E. Processes for Solving Problems
1. People find their daily tasks more meaningful and satisfying when they can improve them.
2. The causes of problems, or the key factors, are often hidden in the background. Ability to solve problems often involves the ability to isolate them from their backgrounds. There is some substance to the cliché that some persons "can't see the forest for the trees."
3. New procedures are often developed from old ones. Problems should be broken down into manageable parts. New ideas can be adapted from old one.
4. People think differently in problem-solving situations. Using a logical, patterned approach is often useful. One approach found to be useful includes these steps:
   a. Define the problem
   b. Establish objectives
   c. Get the facts
   d. Weigh and decide
   e. Take action
   f. Evaluate action

F. Training for Results
1. Participants respond best when they feel training is important to them.
2. The supervisor has responsibility for the training and development of those who report to him.
3. When training is delegated to others, great care must be exercised to insure the trainer has knowledge, aptitude, and interest for his work as a trainer.
4. Training (learning) of some type goes on continually. The most successful supervisor makes certain the learning contributes in a productive manner to operational goals.
5. New employees are particularly susceptible to training. Older employees facing new job situations require specific training, as well as having need for development and growth opportunities.
6. Training needs require continuous monitoring.
7. The training officer of an agency is a professional with a responsibility to assist supervisors in solving training problems.

8. Many of the self-development steps important to the supervisor's own growth are equally important to the development of peers and subordinates. Knowledge of these is important when the supervisor consults with others on development and growth opportunities.

G. Health, Safety, and Accident Prevention
1. Management-minded supervisors take appropriate measures to assist employees in maintaining health and in assuring safe practices in the work environment.
2. Effective safety training and practices help to avoid injury and accidents.
3. Safety should be a management goal. All infractions of safety which are observed should be corrected without exception.
4. Employees' safety attitude, training and instruction, provision of safe tools and equipment, supervision, and leadership are considered highly important factors which contribute to safety and which can be influenced directly by supervisors.
5. When accidents do occur, they should be investigated promptly for very important reasons, including the fact that information which is gained can be used to prevent accidents in the future.

H. Equal Employment Opportunity
1. The supervisor should endeavor to treat all employees fairly, without regard to religion, race, sex, or national origin.
2. Groups tend to reflect the attitude of the leader. Prejudice can be detected even in very subtle form. Supervisors must strive to create a feeling of mutual respect and confidence in every employee.
3. Complete utilization of all human resources is a national goal. Equitable consideration should be accorded women in the work force, minority-group members, the physically and mentally handicapped, and the older employee. The important question is: "Who can do the job?"
4. Training opportunities, recognition for performance, overtime assignments, promotional opportunities, and all other personnel actions are to be handled on an equitable basis.

I. Improving Communications
1. Communications is achieving understanding between the sender and the receiver of a message. It also means sharing information—the creation of understanding.
2. Communication is basic to all human activity. Words are means of conveying meanings; however, real meanings are in people.
3. There are very practical differences in the effectiveness of one-way, impersonal, and two-way communications. Words spoken face-to-face are better understood. Telephone conversations are effective, but lack the rapport of person-to-person exchanges. The whole person communicates.
4. Cooperation and communication in an organization go hand in hand. When there is a mutual respect between people, spelling out rules and procedures for communicating is unnecessary.
5. There are several barriers to effective communications. These include failure to listen with respect and understanding, lack of skill in feedback, and misinterpreting the meanings of words used by the speaker. It is also common

practice to listen to what we want to hear, and tune out things we do not want to hear.
6. Communication is management's chief problem. The supervisor should accept the challenge to communicate more effectively and to improve interagency and intra-agency communications.
7. The supervisor may often plan for and conduct meetings. The planning phase is critical and may determine the success or the failure of a meeting.
8. Speaking before groups usually requires extra effort. Stage fright may never disappear completely, but it can be controlled.

J. Self-Development
1. Every employee is responsible for his own self-development.
2. Toastmaster and toastmistress clubs offer opportunities to improve skills in oral communications.
3. Planning for one's own self-development is of vital importance. Supervisors know their own strengths and limitations better than anyone else.
4. Many opportunities are open to aid the supervisor in his developmental efforts, including job assignments; training opportunities, both governmental and non-governmental—to include universities and professional conferences and seminars.
5. Programmed instruction offers a means of studying at one's own rate.
6. Where difficulties may arise from a supervisor's being away from his work for training, he may participate in televised home study or correspondence courses to meet his self-development needs.

K. Teaching and Training
1. The Teaching Process
Teaching is encouraging and guiding the learning activities of students toward established goals. In most cases this process consists of five steps: preparation, presentation, summarization, evaluation, and application.

   a. Preparation
   Preparation is two-fold in nature; that of the supervisor and the employee. Preparation by the supervisor is absolutely essential to success. He must know what, when, where, how, and whom he will teach. Some of the factors that should be considered are:
   1) The objectives
   2) The materials needed
   3) The methods to be used
   4) Employee participation
   5) Employee interest
   6) Training aids
   7) Evaluation
   8) Summarization

   Employee preparation consists in preparing the employee to receive the material. Probably the most important single factor in the preparation of the employee is arousing and maintaining his interest. He must know the objectives of the training, why he is there, how the material can be used, and its importance to him.

b. Presentation
In presentation, have a carefully designed plan and follow it. The plan should be accurate and complete, yet flexible enough to meet situations as they arise. The method of presentation will be determined by the particular situation and objectives.

c. Summary
A summary should be made at the end of every training unit and program. In addition, there may be internal summaries depending on the nature of the material being taught. The important thing is that the trainee must always be able to understand how each part of the new material relates to the whole.

d. Application
The supervisor must arrange work so the employee will be given a chance to apply new knowledge or skills while the material is still clear in his mind and interest is high. The trainee does not really know whether he has learned the material until he has been given a chance to apply it. If the material is not applied, it loses most of its value.

e. Evaluation
The purpose of all training is to promote learning. To determine whether the training has been a success or failure, the supervisor must evaluate this learning.
In the broadest sense, evaluation includes all the devices, methods, skills, and techniques used by the supervisor to keep himself and the employees informed as to their progress toward the objectives they are pursuing. The extent to which the employee has mastered the knowledge, skills, and abilities, or changed his attitudes, as determined by the program objectives, is the extent to which instruction has succeeded or failed.
Evaluation should not be confined to the end of the lesson, day, or program but should be used continuously. We shall note later the way this relates to the rest of the teaching process.

2. Teaching Methods
A teaching method is a pattern of identifiable student and instructor activity used in presenting training material.
All supervisors are faced with the problem of deciding which method should be used at a given time.

a. Lecture
The lecture is direct oral presentation of material by the supervisor. The present trend is to place less emphasis on the trainer's activity and more on that of the trainee.

b. Discussion
Teaching by discussion or conference involves using questions and other techniques to arouse interest and focus attention upon certain areas, and by doing so creating a learning situation. This can be one of the most

valuable methods because it gives the employees an opportunity to express their ideas and pool their knowledge.

    c. Demonstration
The demonstration is used to teach how something works or how to do something. It can be used to show a principle or what the results of a series of actions will be. A well-staged demonstration is particularly effective because it shows proper methods of performance in a realistic manner.

    d. Performance
Performance is one of the most fundamental of all learning techniques or teaching methods. The trainee may be able to tell how a specific operation should be performed but he cannot be sure he knows how to perform the operation until he has done so.
As with all methods, there are certain advantages and disadvantages to each method.

    e. Which Method to Use
Moreover, there are other methods and techniques of teaching. It is difficult to use any method without other methods entering into it. In any learning situation, a combination of methods is usually more effective than any one method alone.

Finally, evaluation must be integrated into the other aspects of the teaching-learning process.

It must be used in the motivation of the trainees; it must be used to assist in developing understanding during the training; and it must be related to employee application of the results of training.

This is distinctly the role of the supervisor.